BY MRS. KEMPER CAMPBELL

Here I Raise Mine Ebenezer
Whom God Hath Joined Asunder . . .
Marching Without Banners
Words to the Unwise

Words to the Unwise

CAUTIONARY TALES
By *Mrs. Kemper Campbell*

Litta B. H. Campbell

SIMON AND SCHUSTER : NEW YORK

All rights reserved
including the right of reproduction
in whole or in part in any form
Copyright © 1971 by Mrs. Kemper Campbell
Published by Simon and Schuster
Rockefeller Center, 630 Fifth Avenue
New York, New York 10020

First printing

SBN 671-21022-X
Library of Congress Catalog Card Number: 75-159126
Designed by Irving Perkins
Manufactured in the United States of America
by H. Wolff Book Mfg. Co., Inc., New York, N.Y.

FOR LOLA, *sister and steadfast friend*

CONTENTS

A Word of Preface: Back Again

MY BELATED success, such as it is, has led to many disappointments among my friends. No doubt their efforts are as worthy as mine, but chance has favored me and they are doomed to failure.

I cannot help them as much as I would like to. My agent is retiring, and I have no influence with my publishers—only a deep gratitude to them. In the words of Jessie Rittenhouse:

Oh where is the appraiser
Who can the claim compute
Of him who makes you sing again
When all your songs were mute?

Or where is he can reckon
The debt when all is said
Of him who makes you dream again
When all your dreams were dead?

Even successful authors have a portfolio of rejection slips. The American Express agent in our town came to recognize my manuscripts when they were returned. He was a taciturn man. I always dreaded it when he handed me the package with the remark, "It's back again." I was glad when American Express closed its Victorville office and I had to go thirty miles to Barstow, where I was unknown.

The only valid reason for writing is the joy to be found in words. It is like to the joy some people find in playing the piano and others find in painting for pleasure. I should have continued to write all my life just for the love of it even if I had never found a publisher.

I once carried a friend's manuscript to London. The author thought it would appeal to an English agent. I did my best but the manuscript preceded me home.

This same friend was indignant because Mother's Day verses she had written for a dead mother were rejected. The publisher explained, "Few people send cards to dead mothers."

A Family Affair

THIS RANCH has been the family blessing and the family curse. My son would have been better off financially if he had accepted an offer to join a law firm in Los Angeles. My son-in-law, a graduate engineer, would have made more money if he had gone with Lockheed. No one wants to trade the ranch for city living. The same problem confronts my five grandchildren.

Living so close together is not always easy. We are trying to accomplish the impossible. There is a widespread notion that families cannot live close together.

We have just passed a family crisis. Florida Scott Maxwell says in her book *The Days of My Years*, "I tread lightly on the eggshells of my children's affections." Well, this last month I broke through one or two shells. There is no mountain higher than the mountain that started out as a molehill.

Irritations accumulated to the danger point.

First, by way of explanation, I sort the mail. I think that anything written on a postcard is in the field of public domain and the subject of fair comment. This is not universally accepted. There were objections to my reading the incoming and outgoing postcards. My defense was that postcards are an index to whether our guests are pleased.

Their comments on the food, the riding horses and related subjects were helpful.

Once we had a houseful of guests who came to the ranch year after year. They wrote a series of cards in different foreign languages. I read only English. Each card contained one phrase that was meant to arouse my curiosity—"Mrs. Campbell's fruit soup," "the food this year," "Mrs. Campbell's hair," or "you would never believe it." The rest of the card was in Swedish or French or some other alien tongue. This should have curbed my practice of reading postcards.

Another complaint was the manner in which I answered the telephone. When I gave up my law practice and retired to private life I wanted to answer the phone by simply saying "Hello" not "Kemper Campbell Ranch, Mrs. Kemper Campbell speaking," which is both dignified and business-like.

And last of all there were the menus. My daughter-in-law and my daughter are both excellent cooks. Not only are they excellent cooks but they are curious about food and eager to try new recipes. They have a reputation to maintain. Sometimes I think they are like my mother who used to say, "I want a change even if it is for the worse."

I prefer a good beef stew to beef stroganoff, and so do many of my friends.

The air was charged with static. Any life is better than persistent static.

I am incapable of continued unhappiness. I cannot sleep unless I know what I am going to do "just in case." I have never fallen between two jobs; if one horse is exhausted I have another one saddled and bridled and ready to ride.

And so I worked out an alternate plan for the future. Some of the details were intriguing—the more I thought about it the more I liked it. I persuaded myself that I would have peace and quiet, something I had never had in my life before and never wanted. I knew I would miss the birds and the beasts and the sounds of the ranch which are music to my ears. It made me sad to think that the birds and the beasts would not miss me but would go on living just as though I were watching over them. I resolved not to miss my family—let them miss me. I was too deep in the forest to see the trees.

Alas, I waited too long. Before the hour I had set for my departure everything fell into its proper perspective. Time brought compromise and compromise ended in harmony.

The King said, "I shall never forget it." The White Queen answered, "You will unless you make a memorandum of it."

I remembered what a wise nephew once said to me. "You cannot demand respect; you can only command it."

So I have an elaborate plan for a new life which I will never use. I shall lay it away with the plans for the houses that I never built.

I have a devoted family—that is to say, they watch over me, they tell me when I sit down in something, if I am ill or in need they overwhelm me with their kindness and concern, but if someone shot me they would simply say, "Well, what did you expect?"

Confessions

THERE ARE two sound reasons for memorializing one's faults. Once you have admitted to them, friends are on notice and can avoid trouble. And when you have defined them, there is a hint of repentance.

These traits or sins, depending on your side of the shield, are uniquely mine—not one of my children has inherited them, and my friends do not sympathize with them. First, I do not cut my flowers. I want to see them growing in the garden. It makes me sad to pick them and then find them fading as soon as my back is turned. And since I do not pick my flowers I do not want anyone else to pick them.

Once I tended a peony with great care. It was the first peony I had raised on the desert. Finally it had one promising pink bud. On a Thursday my cook phoned to tell me the awful truth. A guest had picked my peony. My anger was greater than her offense. She saw me when I came home for the weekend and threw the flower into the toilet and pulled the chain. I never even saw the flower in full bloom. But I forgave her when she wrote a penitent letter. She had looked all over Los Angeles for a replacement. Not one was to be found. She had mistaken the peony for a rose to wear in her hair.

My next failing is harder to define. I do not like people to take my friends. People go shopping for friends as they would go to a dress shop. "I like this one," they say, and they extend uncalled-for kindnesses which cannot be ignored. I will divide my acquaintances with anyone—even strangers. But I am jealous of my intimate friends. I do not want many close friends; they are a blessing and an obligation. I find that I can only encircle a dozen or so with my love and protection. You are welcome to borrow my books, anyone can use my car, but I do not want to share my friends except with each other. My conduct is indefensible. It does not even endear me to the friends I have. I do not recommend this attitude.

And last of all, I boast of my few generosities. I am never the "anonymous giver." In spite of what the Bible says about not letting your right hand know what your left hand does, I keep my right hand well-informed.

There was a great woman who lived in Victorville. After she died it became known that she had helped many of our neighbors. She had paid to have a little boy's clubfeet corrected. She had buried a lone Indian widow beside her husband. She had kept a hard-working man from losing his home because his wife was ill. She had boasted of none of these things and she had sworn the recipients to secrecy while she lived. The village loved her and called a school by her name. They will never do this for me.

I confess to these vices not to distinguish myself from all the other people I know but to warn them against the same failings. Let them discover their own faults and not copy mine. I wouldn't like that. I'm sure there is no danger. "There never was a hunchback by persuasion."

I am not truly repentant. I am like a boy I grew up with

so very long ago. He was engaged to a devout Christian girl. She persuaded him to attend a revival service. The minister asked those who wanted to be saved to stand up. The boy stood up and asked them to pray for him so that he would want to be saved. He said that so far he had no interest in salvation.

Charity

MY RELIGION has been severely tested. Do I really believe in the teaching of Christ and does it do me good to go to church?

Friday night a man ran his car off the road just outside my bedroom window. It was two-thirty in the morning and he persisted in racing his motor until the wheels were in the sand down to the hubs. Then in the eerie light of the gas lamps I saw him stagger past my window, smoking a cigar. Later, he returned to torture his engine again.

At last I called the sheriff's office and three cars responded. Jean came with them. By then the man was asleep in the car.

My daughter recognized him and told the officers they could go back to the station. She took the drunken man to a room and saw him comfortable for the night. He was still in bed when I went to church at eleven o'clock.

Now I have never had any affection for the man. He

went from Victorville to the penitentiary where he be-longed. I do not know how long he served. I have heard men say he would give you his last ten dollars, but that does not endear him to me since he never had his last ten dollars. When he is not being supported by the state, he lives largely on those who know him, and the longer you have known him the more he feels free to ask for a loan.

He usually calls on his friends just before lunch or just before dinner. I think he goes without breakfast. He knows so many kind-hearted people that he is in no danger of starving.

I went to church with the full intention of telling him to be gone as soon as I returned. I had seen enough of him, and I proposed to tell him so and tell him not to darken my door again.

Alas, the minister chose as his text 1 Corinthians 13–3: "And though I bestow all my goods to feed the poor, and though I give my body to be burned, and have not charity, it profiteth me nothing."

The minister went on and on for the better part of an hour. He read the first eight verses of the chapter. He talked about how "charity endureth all things," "charity never faileth," and "though I have all faith so that I could move mountains and have not charity, I am as nothing."

That was three days ago. The man is still with us.

Breakfast with Strangers

I HAD an experience a few nights ago that I hope will never happen to me again. I planned to spend the night with my sister after the theater. I tried to follow her home in my car, but I lost my way. Finally I was confronted by a row of flats that all looked alike. A light was burning in one of the flats so I drove into the garage. It appeared familiar, but when I went up the back stairs I found a strange refrigerator on the landing.

It was late at night and I was frightened. I rapped on the back door and an old man in a long nightshirt answered my knock reluctantly. I could hardly blame him. My story was that I did not know where my sister lived, and I asked to see the telephone book. I was almost in tears. The man disappeared and returned with his wife in a matching nightgown. I assured them that I was not a member of a band of thieves but an old lady in need of help. They opened the door and stood one on each side of me as I found the number.

I drove to the right apartment house, but when I reached for my suitcase, alas, I had left it on the other porch. I did not know the number of the other apartment nor the name of the people who lived there.

There must be an angel assigned to watch over stupid people. The next morning I wandered up and down the street until I found a palm tree in the middle of a driveway. I remembered the palm.

The little old man and woman were delighted to see me by daylight and insisted that I share their ample breakfast.

No Answer

I HAD an automobile accident last month. This is how it happened. I was going down the ramp from the parking lot in front of the post office. There was a car directly in front of me. I stepped on the gas instead of the brake. I suppose other drivers have done this before, but it had never happened to me.

I had one second to decide whether to hit the car in front of me and push it into the oncoming traffic and thus be involved in litigation for the rest of my life, or to commit suicide. I decided on suicide.

The result of the decision was far better than I had any reason to hope. Damage to my car and to the property of the Federal government amounted to a total of $252, which I willingly paid without troubling the already overburdened insurance companies. The only permanent damage was to my pride.

The local postmaster, who is a friend of mine, was looking out of the window as I left the parking lot. He said to a stranger sitting beside him, "There goes the smartest woman in town."

The stranger looked out to see me go through two low brick walls and an iron fence. "And what makes you think so?" he asked.

Do Plants Love Us?

Is IT possible that plants know how we feel about them and respond to kindness?

I saw an experiment on television which was truly remarkable. I am too old to be easily convinced by magic; I am disinclined to believe that the plants in my window know how I complain of their ingratitude. I would be embarrassed to go near the window. But I must admit I have personally seen evidence of this fantastic theory. Since I read an article on the subject and saw the show on television, I have been more careful about what I say in the hearing of my African violets. Last year I threatened to put them out in the cold. This year they are doing much better, and I thank them each time I give them water.

And there is the story of the white cyclamen. One day my daughter and I had a disagreement—we never call a disagreement a quarrel. Quarrels are harder to forget. Apologies only underwrite the unpleasantness. I can't bear to have a continuing strangeness between us, so I sent her a beautiful white cyclamen assuring her of my love.

The flowers faded and I told Jean to discard them—that cyclamens never bloomed again. But she kept the plant and the next year it was more beautiful than ever. I had never seen such a lovely cyclamen.

She sent the plant back to me with a message of affection. And again I told her the plant would never bloom again. They never do for me. She kept it the third year. This year, while Jean is in Europe, it is a vision of white blossoms reminding me of her each morning. Can it be that it is responding year by year to the love it symbolizes?

Too Easily Offended

MUST WE be cautious when we talk to or about animals? How much do they understand and do they react to our displeasure?

I remember once when Rex Duncan and Rin-Tin-Tin were guests on the ranch. Rex gave Rin-Tin-Tin difficult commands which the dog obeyed with surprising intelligence. I thought the show had gone on long enough. I said, "Don't ask him to do any more, let him rest. He looks tired." Rin-Tin-Tin promptly came across the room and laid his head on my lap.

My granddaughter Celeste had a patient, popular dog that had never been unkind to anyone. Then she raised a baby sparrow. The bird slept in her room and followed her during the day. The dog rejected both Celeste and the bird. He had been used to sleeping in Celeste's room. He took to sleeping on the porch. He simply refused to share Celeste's affections with a bird. One day they were left alone on the front lawn. It was a tragedy. The dog killed the bird and hid in the bushes. Ever after that day when he heard the word "bird" he hid in the bushes.

A truthful friend told this story. She grew up on a ranch in New Mexico. There were rattlesnakes around the barn and chicken pens. An Indian worked for her father. One day her father told the Indian to hunt the snakes out of their holes.

The Indian protested. "No," he said, "the snakes are our friends."

"Then tell your friends to go somewhere else," the father replied.

The Indian went to each hole and talked softly in his native tongue. After that no snakes were found within several hundred yards of the house or barn. My friend is so trustworthy, I find it hard to doubt her word.

Once I knew two sisters who both worked in offices. They had a plague of stubborn mice in their house. One day the older of the two wrote a courteous letter to the mice. She said that she and her sister were both away from home all day and could not give their guests the service they required. She suggested that they move to the home of her employer, whom she disliked very much. She pointed out that this man had a large house and plenty of help and assured the mice they would be very comfortable. Within a week the man complained of an invasion of mice.

I don't want to believe these stories, but they were all told to me by honest friends. Animals should not be so easily offended by what we say. We have to ride our tongues with a curb when we talk about other people; I should like to speak freely about dogs and cats and birds and other animals without fear of hurting their feelings.

Snakes, Just Snakes

IF YOU want the undivided attention of an audience just talk about snakes. No one will interrupt you unless he has a better story to tell.

People wrongly associate rattlesnakes with the desert. Mr. Henderson, who wrote *Sand and Solitude*, says that he has seen more rattlesnakes in one week in the hills back of Laguna than he has seen in ten years on the desert.

One of the first questions strangers ask when they come to the ranch is "Do you have rattlesnakes?" Until last summer the answer was "Not really." Last summer a mother brought her eleven-year-old daughter for a visit. She asked the usual question and Jean assured her there was no danger. She said she had lived on the ranch for forty years, and in all that time she had seen only one rattler and it was about five inches long. The mother replied that her child was a loner and "If there is a rattler on the ranch, she will find it." And find it she did.

One night the child and her father were walking along the road in front of the lawns. A cat was stalking something in the grass.

"See that cat," the child said. "He is following a rattler."

"Don't be foolish," the father replied. "There are no rattlers here."

"There is one over there. See that cat."

She was right. We have had to revise our answer to the usual question to include that one snake.

I can befriend almost any animal but a snake. I have come to terms with rabbits, I defend coyotes and protect kit foxes. I have even learned to enjoy lizards. In fact there is one growing up in my closet now. What he eats is a mystery, but he appears to thrive on it. But what ecologist can prove that snakes serve any useful purpose except to remind us of sin? I mistrust anyone who makes a pet of a snake. In my own paraphrase of Ella Wheeler Wilcox:

In whose breast there lurks no dread,
There lurks the serpent's nature there instead.

My neighbors Mr. and Mrs. Cole had an adventure last spring. They live on the desert closer to the mountains than we do. They have a glassed-in porch where they can watch the birds on the feeders. One morning Mr. Cole stepped on to the porch to look for the mountain bluebirds. He was startled to see a mouse running across the floor pursued by a sidewinder—the smallest and one of the deadliest rattlers. The snake had been hibernating under the couch and had felt the warm March sun. He was hungry.

I am happy to report that Mr. Cole shot the snake and the mouse got away. It was only a tiny field mouse with little round ears.

There was a man in Victorville who divorced his wife because he would not share their home with a boa constrictor. He was not a bad husband, but his stepsons refused to give up the snake. I think the wife made a mistake. The boa will outgrow the house, but the man might have been around for a long time.

Last week a boa constrictor made headlines across the country. A man had bought a house in South Los Angeles. He was surprised to see a snake raise its head in the toilet bowl. He flushed the toilet and shortly thereafter it came up in the toilet across the hall. The police arrived and nothing happened. They suspected the man of being demented. But the second time they were called they found the snake. It was a five-foot boa constrictor. Apparently the former owner had tried to dispose of it by flushing it down the toilet.

No one who hears this story will ever forget it. It will have a permanent place in his memory. The bathroom will be a constant reminder.

Some good stories have no moral, but this story has one: Never flush a boa constrictor down a toilet.

The Car with the Gold Initials

THERE IS no markup in marrying for money—at least not
with men. Women who marry for money have a better
chance of success. Husbands are inclined to be proud and
liberal, and besides they die first. Wives always outlive their
husbands and have a few years to enjoy his beneficence,
which they have frequently earned.

Men are less fortunate. When the Darby and Joan days
have passed, wives change. They begin to suspect that their
husbands married them for money and not for love. It is the
fly caught in the amber. All women want to feel that they
are loved for themselves alone, which, of course, is seldom
true.

Earl and Florence and I attended Andrews University at
the same time. They were in love, or so I assumed. Certainly Florence was in love with Earl. She was a beautiful
and resourceful girl. I remember once when a group including Earl and Florence were on an outing. I think we were
taking the train from Berrien Springs to St. Joseph. I have
forgotten most of the details, but I do remember one incident that happened. Earl was to board the train at a whistle
stop along the way. Florence discovered that the train did
not make that stop, so as we neared the station Florence
pulled the emergency cord. The train stopped and Earl
joined us. He was pleased, but the conductor was very
angry.

Earl came to California soon after I did. I waited for him to send for Florence, but instead he married a widow with a million dollars and two sons. The million dollars weighed heavily against his love for Florence. I never heard from Florence again. I hope she married a man worthy of her devotion.

Earl took very readily to his new life. They built a beautiful home and he drove a luxury car with his initials in gold letters on the door.

I drew up their mutual wills leaving everything to each other. It was not an even trade. Earl's estate consisted mostly of love and affection.

Years passed and the wife died after a lingering illness.

I shall never forget the day that Earl brought her will to the office. He was a stricken man. She had opened the safe deposit box and torn her signature from her will. He had always assumed that his wife loved him. He could not understand how any woman could reject him.

There was nothing I could do to restore the mutilated will. The estate was all separate property and it was distributed to her sons under a former will.

Fortunately that is not the end of the story.

Earl had been a good stepfather and the boys provided him with a modest living. He moved into a small apartment, but he never again drove a car with gold initials.

So Like a Husband

BETSY AND I were discussing the hazards of traveling in Europe—especially traveling by train. European trains are nervous. They have a habit of disregarding the time and leaving ahead of schedule. It is very annoying.

Betsy had an aunt who spent her whole life taking care of her mother who was more than adequate to take care of herself. Once when they were traveling from Austria to Dijon, France, the daughter stepped off the train to make a purchase. The train thoughtlessly moved on without her. Betsy's grandmother was not disturbed. Instead she welcomed the opportunity to be alone the rest of the journey. She looked about the compartment for something to read and in her daughter's suitcase she found a book wrapped in a French newspaper. It was *Lady Chatterley's Lover*. Neither one spoke to the other for a week.

They say that someone misses every train. It was the judge who missed the train from Zurich to Interlaken. We were on a trip across Europe with the judge and his wife. The judge became intrigued by a tunnel near the tracks and he was deep inside the dark tunnel when the train moved out of the station.

When we reached Interlaken I insisted on sitting down by the bereft wife. My husband pointed out that there was no way the judge could get out of Switzerland without coming up that certain stairway and through a hole in the platform. And he also pointed out that if we waited we would miss our train to Milan.

But I could not leave the poor wife sans husband, sans money, and worst of all, sans passport.

So we sat and watched for that familiar head to emerge from the hole in the floor. It was exciting, like hunting wild game.

At last he came. I expected to see a tearful reunion. Not so. The judge's greeting was frigid, even for Switzerland. "Why didn't you wait for me?" he demanded.

A Total Loss

I AM wary of the new California divorce laws. Divorce is now less involved than marriage. Instead of infidelity, drunkenness, cruelty and the like, it takes only a fancy or a whim. The judge has no choice. He has but to say the word.

I have had sad news today. Two friends who have been married for five years, happily I think, have decided to get a divorce. They are both teachers in the same high school —intelligent and attractive. I have heard only the wife's story.

With a summer vacation to enjoy they chose an ocean

cruise. It was a mistake. Eight weeks is too long to be confined with twelve passengers—the same twelve passengers day after day.

They were bored. They had never before spent so much time alone. There was nothing to talk about and nothing to do. As a result two unfortunate things happened. The wife got pregnant, and she told her husband that she had had a lover before they were married.

She chose the wrong time to reveal her past. She should have warned him, if ever, before their marriage. After five years it was too late. She was too sure of his love. But secrets are seldom kept forever. "The secret you possess now possesses you."

The husband wants a divorce. I do not justify him. This too could be forgiven and forgotten. The wife was foolish to believe that her confession would make no difference to her husband. One generation cannot annul the sacred ban of many centuries. Virtue is still a priceless asset, even in a modern marriage.

Nevertheless I shall desert my typewriter and go to the husband. I shall plead for time and then for mercy. I shall compute for him the losses he will suffer. There is the loyalty of her family. They have been exceedingly kind to him. He can rely on them whenever they are needed. Not only will the property be divided between them, but they must divide their friends—these to go with the wife and those for the husband. And there is the accumulation of happy memories that both must fold away and forget. They have built a common language which must be discarded. It is all a total loss, and for what? There was no insurance on the marriage—there never is.

I shall warn the husband with complete assurance that what Andrew Lang said long ago is still true: "No man but loves what he has lost."

Gifts

IT IS always disappointing to receive a present from someone whom you have been trying for years to forget. Presents cannot be ignored, and presents are sometimes a cheap substitute for responsibility.

I know a family with four grown children. The parents are in daily need of help. The two sons and one daughter provide them with the necessities to keep them comfortable. The fourth daughter brings her mother an orchid and a kiss on Christmas and on her birthday. She is the favorite daughter. Well, there was the prodigal son. Who has ever been able to justify his father's attitude?

Maggie is a friend we have left over from the Second World War. She was untiring in her efforts to marry Henry. She did her best to make a man of him after the army gave up. She took the little money we gave her for Christmas to buy vitamin pills for Henry. The effect was negligible.

Maggie never stopped working except for a week when a

baby was born. Henry followed along in his quiet, ineffectual way. But anyone with Maggie's industry and ambition was bound to succeed. Now she owns her own laundromat.

Henry had one handicap which made Maggie unhappy. Henry could not dance. Maggie is a pearl, though not a cultured one, and her only contact with the arts is her elegant dancing. She dances divinely.

Henry worried about his inability to dance. He has many other shortcomings, but this is the only one he recognizes. Last year he earned a few hundred dollars. With this money he bought five hundred dollars' worth of dancing lessons and gave the receipt to Maggie for Christmas.

"For You Departed"

ALAN PATON has recently written a touching memorial to his wife, *For You Departed*. He relates one experience which should reassure troubled wives.

He tells how he was once involved with a younger woman. Mrs. Paton asked him if he was in love with Joan. He gave her an honest reply.

"Yes," he said, "I am, but I do not want to marry her. Only let me go to Cape Town and say goodbye."

Mrs. Paton replied, "You may go and when you return I will make it up to you." She kept her word. How wise she was.

It is so very hard to do nothing when suspicion points to another woman. It is not exactly a question of patience—it's just silence and holding to the daily routine. Time is on the side of the wife. Weeks and months pass—the glamour pales. The husband tires of playing the game and is ready to dismiss the whole affair from his mind.

So many wives make haste to destroy their own happiness.

There was the woman I knew who found out that her husband was involved in a secret love affair. She ordered him out of the house. He was reluctant to go, but she insisted, and she helped him to pack. He left and her heart broke.

She talked about her husband much of the time. She told me over and over again how handsome he was. I sympathize with women who are married to handsome men; I do not envy women whose husbands have no attraction for other women—safe but deadly.

One day I said to my husband, "You are really not the most handsome man in Los Angeles." He was only amused.

"Well, who is?" he inquired. I could not think of another man.

The woman is dead so the story can be told. She was shot and killed by an unknown assailant—a friend or a foe. She was always attracted to handsome men. More than one wife confided her fears to me.

My husband was briefly the object of her roving affections. She was no half-hearted siren. That winter Kemper had to make frequent trips to Sacramento. She would plan to board the midnight train at San Fernando, the first stop beyond Los Angeles.

One night she was disappointed to find me on the same train. We registered at the same hotel in Sacramento. During the morning she met me in the Ladies' Room and grabbed my purse. "I will not return the purse until you agree to talk to me," she said.

I never conferred with my husband's friends. "Keep the purse," I answered. "It contains nothing of value." Of course she followed me into the lobby and returned the purse.

That ended the friendship. Kemper did not approve of women who snatched his wife's purse. I never knew whether my husband was completely innocent. "Only the Arabian bird lives chaste because there is but one."

That night we were not on the train to Los Angeles. Kemper suggested that we take the *Old River Queen* down the Sacramento to San Francisco. We never left our stateroom. Kemper ordered supper, and they brought us crisp bacon and toast and marmalade and tea.

Oh, my darling! The memory of that night still glows when I think of you.

An Eccentric House

ONCE MR. CAMPBELL gave me a check for $2500. "You may want to do something one day that I won't approve of, and here is the money to do it," he said.

Months passed before I felt an urge to spend the money. And then I dreamed of a little house, compact, convenient and inexpensive. It was such a house as I had never seen—an experimental house like no other house that had ever been built.

The house looked like a Flemish cottage, but the interior was revolutionary. The kitchen had a vent so that it could be hosed out to save endless scrubbing. There were zinc-lined drawers opening from the dining room into the kitchen. Before dinner was served one drawer held the salads and one the desserts. I could serve them from the end of the dining table where I sat, and I could replace them with the dishes to be washed later. The three drawers contained the used dishes, and the kitchen was clean and tidy when the meal ended. There was no waiting on table, no traveling from dining room to kitchen. Sitting at the end of the table, I had only to open and close drawers that moved quietly on polished runners.

The beds were all balanced on swivels and stood up when not in use. It was easy to keep the bedrooms clean, and there was space for other activities besides sleeping.

The wall between the kitchen and the bathroom had a

shelf for each member of the family. As I ironed in the kitchen I had only to open a door above the ironing board and place each child's freshly ironed clothes on his shelf to be taken out in the bathroom as needed.

I was very proud of this house. It kept itself clean like a hound's tooth.

My sister built a house at the same time. It was built for an investment, and she did not intend it to be a permanent home. It was a conventional house, and I once remarked that I would lose my mind in a house with so much gilt and glitter.

Our circumstances changed and reluctantly I sold the house and moved to Hollywood. And then the irony of it—the man who bought my house lost his mind and spent months in an institution. He could never work the combination.

An Angry Will

A CLOSE friend of mine died recently and left his affairs in utter confusion. I am glad I do not represent the estate. The lawyer charged with this duty will earn his fee and much more, which is frequently the case.

The man lived alone and had plenty of time and intelligence to make a simple will expressing his wishes and let it go at that. Instead he had purchased a book on how to avoid probate. The book should be called "How to avoid probate and get into all kinds of trouble."

I have practiced law for half a century, and if I knew of any way to avoid probate I should be quick to take advantage of it.

Of course there is one way to avoid both probate and inheritance tax. One can give away everything he owns. The law looks with favor on such generosity, providing the gift tax is paid. But the gift must be outright. I remember the woman in Pasadena who gave her son an apartment house, or thought she did. She reserved the right to a part of the income and the pleasure of redecorating the place at will. The courts held that it was not a valid gift and exacted the inheritance tax. And even more unfortunate was the case of the magnanimous husband who gave his bride half his wealth. Unfortunately she died first and he had to pay inheritance tax on his princely gift.

I attended a wedding recently. It was an old-fashioned service and the groom said solemnly, "With all my worldly goods I thee endow." I looked about for a man from the Internal Revenue Service; surely the groom should pay a gift tax. Here is a source of revenue which has been overlooked by the government.

My friend left many notes about what he intended to do with his money and other possessions, but none of them were valid. Unfortunately he left an old will written in anger at a time when he had just concluded his second divorce, and he took the occasion to make a public statement about his wives. It was all unnecessary. Neither exwife had any legal right to his estate and only a casual interest in his sentiments about her. He had later learned to live with his loss, and the fire of his anger had flickered and gone out.

Wills should be written with wisdom and kindliness. No man can speak from the grave. A dead man cannot correct his mistakes or alter his bequests. If the testator has reason to disinherit anyone, let it be by silence—or by the gift of a dollar. An unanswered question is punishment enough.

Let no man draw an angry will. I learned this lesson from a will that came to our office a long time ago, which read: "I leave nothing to my son and utterly disinherit him in return for the beating he gave me last Thanksgiving." What a savage will to become a public document and to tarnish the son's name forever.

Unscrupulous Generosity

LEAVING ONE wife and marrying another may be forgiven, but a father who disinherits his children in favor of a second or third or fourth wife is guilty of a sin which should blacken his name as long as he is remembered.

The mother dies, leaving her entire estate to her husband. It may have been her sole and separate property. She loves her husband, believes in him, and trusts him to do right by their children.

After a time he marries again—marries a young and attractive woman. And he throws his wealth into the balance to span the gap between them. The husband dies first just as the young wife expected (husbands are inclined to die first), and she is left a wealthy widow.

This is no exaggeration. Ask any lawyer or any banker.

In my time I have known two men who became millionaires by wisely investing the first wife's money. They were old and the second wives were young and greedy. Old men avoid trouble; they are done with quarreling. And the wives made solemn promises. "Can't you trust me to do right by 'our' children?" they asked. "You know I will take care of the children."

And so they do. One of these wives gives each of the four children one hundred dollars for Christmas. She inherited a million dollars from their father. The other wife was equally rich. When she died she left the two daughters a thousand dollars apiece. This was how these women kept their solemn promises.

I have seldom felt that a new law was needed or would be of any benefit, but such injustice should be legally prohibited. Laws have been passed forbidding a man to make a will ignoring his family in favor of a church. This law should include disinheriting his children in favor of a second wife.

Making a will is a privilege, not a right. It is the duty of the state to control a man's property after his death since it is no longer his. No man can speak from the tomb.

There are things no old man should be allowed to do.

Making a will is one of them. Let him revoke a will if he desires, but thereafter let the laws of inheritance prevail.

A Purpose in Life

IT VEXES me to hear anyone say, "I might as well be dead." I am not in accord with this abstract supposition. There is no proof that one would be better off dead since no one who has tried it has returned to make a report.

I have a friend who has said she would be better off dead many times too often. In fact to say it once is to say it too often. I thought about her circumstances and I decided to give her something to live for. I enjoy her friendship and I want her to be happy. It is true that she has raised and educated her children and they are self-supporting. They are good parents and her grandchildren are well cared for. No one of them has left his or her husband or wife and brought her a second family to care for. This is sometimes an incentive to live.

It occurred to me that her finances were in something of a bungle. She had received bad advice from her lawyers. I was one of them. I decided to take her to a wise lawyer in whom I have complete confidence. She is not quite eighty and has enough income from a trust from her father to make her comfortable. She no longer plans to travel. She has seen a fair sample of the world and likes it best where she is.

Sure enough the lawyer found a way by which she could pay a modest gift tax and give her family all of her personal estate. By doing this she has saved them $90,000 in inheritance taxes. The best of the plan is that she has to live five years in order to make the gift valid.

So by just simply living she is worth $1500 a month to her family. She is happy to keep on living for $1500 a month. It's a real bargain. I don't see that the attitude of her family has changed. They were always willing she should live as long as she liked. But her attitude toward life in general has improved. She is enjoying her importance.

She no longer says, "I might as well be dead." She has to take the best care of herself since her death would cost the family $90,000. She still worries for fear she won't make it to eighty-six but that is more cheerful than wishing she were dead.

No Emergency

SAKI ONCE said that some people are infinitely improved by death.

There was the Johnson family that lived fourteen miles out of town. The youngest boy of nine had never seen a train until his father died. My father was with the under-taker when he took the coffin out in which to bury the old man. Before they left, the wife brought an old broom into the room and held it over his dead form. "Now I can have a new broom," she said, not unkindly. It was simply an an-nouncement of her future plans.

After the funeral Mrs. Johnson sold the large farm and moved to town to live comfortably on the fortune her hus-band had left her.

This weekend a doctor friend of mine told me about one of his patients who died recently. The woman had arthritis which she used as a weapon against her husband. She carped at him all day and destroyed his nights. Her pain protected her against any criticism.

One day not long ago the husband called the doctor and said that his wife had not been breathing for half an hour.

"My God," the doctor exclaimed. "She may be dead."

"I thought of that," the husband replied.

Meeting the Inevitable

AT EIGHTY-FOUR I have few complaints against life. But I would suggest one improvement. We can choose a career, choose the place where we prefer to live, single out a hus-band or reject an offer of marriage. But except for death by violent means, which has my qualified approval, the way of our final exit is left to chance. If I had my way I would choose heart trouble. I am working on it with a fair prospect of success. I regard senile dementia as the worst of all fatal illnesses.

Four of my friends have had this misfortune. It is very sad, and saddest of all is the change in personality. One modest, thoughtful woman, whose strongest expression of displeasure was a mild "Oh, sugar," became most profane. One peaceful soul resorted to physical violence. Someone suggested that it was only a repressed desire, but I do not believe that she had wished anyone harm in her whole life.

In time the family is driven to a painful decision. I am trying to help the husband of a dear friend to make this decision. They are with me this weekend, and it is only a matter of time—a very short time. The wife has been a rare person, affectionate and intelligent, but the ruin is complete. I can only comfort the husband by assuring him that as far as I can observe homes for these unfortunate men and women are humane and well-conducted. The ruthless search for scandal has failed to make a case against them.

Senility is not always cruel. These men and women are frequently reconciled to new surroundings with surprising ease. They are comfortable. They feel safe. Many of them have never before had anyone to wait on them. It is a welcome change.

A neighbor's family finally had to send the grandmother away. Later they brought her home for the weekend. When they took her back she drew a long sigh of relief. "It's wonderful to be home again," she said.

A husband had his wife home for Christmas. She was restless all day and begged to be taken back. "I am afraid they will lock me out," she complained.

I knew a prominent lawyer who slowly became incompetent. His wife was very patient, for he deserved limitless kindness. At last she had to face the inevitable. He was a danger to himself and could not be left alone. She took him to a home for the aged. He was so contented that after his first dinner he went to the kitchen and gave his expensive watch to the cook to show his appreciation. He was happy the rest of his life. He believed he owned the institution, and he was increasingly proud of the management.

Give Him Strawberries

PREGNANT WOMEN have lost one of their few advantages. When I was having my family a woman could indulge in any whim. My choice was buttermilk and cantaloupe any time of day or night. Some women had more sophisticated tastes and they demanded and received expensive foods around the clock. This is now forbidden. Doctors tell prospective mothers what to eat and when.

I once knew an old lady who was afraid of dying hungry. Many times she called her daughter at midnight and asked for food. "I don't want to go to Heaven hungry and have to be fed the minute I arrive," she explained.

Santayana said that whenever his father thought he was about to die he called for Extreme Unction and a boiled chicken.

Eduardo Ciannelli told me the story of an old man who lived near his home in Ischia. He was dying and the doctor said his wife could give him anything he wanted. She asked her husband what he craved. "Strawberries, strawberries," he replied. "I have never had enough strawberries."

Strawberries were out of season and Eduardo's mother offered to send to Naples for them.

"Oh, it won't be necessary," the old woman said. "I just mashed up some radishes and put lots of sugar on them and he ate them and enjoyed them. He will die happy."

The Doctors' Dilemma

I TAUGHT in a medical college for over thirty years, and naturally I have a comforting faith in the skill and integrity of doctors. But I sometimes question their judgment.

The most popular doctor in Victorville went on a vacation recently and left his practice in the hands of a stranger. One of his patients, a woman ninety-six years old, was not feeling well one morning and she went to the doctor's office. He put her through every odious examination known to the profession. The result was an inferior case of diabetes—which is the right of every woman past eighty.

The poor woman has not yet recovered from the effects of the examination. She is still in shock. Certainly the age of the patient should be one of the guidelines for the treatment.

A friend was sitting in the office of a well-known surgeon in Los Angeles. The surgeon had a phone call from a former patient who was past seventy-five. She insisted on a long conversation. Finally the surgeon became exasperated. "Mrs. Pendleman," he said firmly, "you do not have syphilis."

Some time ago I read about a woman who wrote to the government for a pamphlet on feminine hygiene. "I think I have it," she said.

No Way Out

I HAVE recently visited a friend who is confined to a hospital for the mentally ill. The doctors give little hope for her recovery.

In a lucid interval she said, "I know what my trouble was. I never faced up to life. When I felt discouraged or depressed I either went to see a psychiatrist or took a pill."

On my sixteenth birthday I was disappointed and disgusted with life. I said to my mother, "I wish I could die." She replied calmly, "Well, that is the only way out of this world that I know of."

I pity sixteen-year-old girls. It is an unhappy time. There is nothing sweet about being sixteen. But I finally learned to trust life, and I have enjoyed its bread and wine for almost seventy years since that doleful day.

I am thankful my mother did not send me to a psychiatrist. I might so easily have formed the habit. I love to talk about myself.

Not Her Cup of Tea

I AM always so happy when she comes to visit us. She is more amusing than the best comic strip, and I regard her in the same light.

She is a graduate nurse and there are none better. Death must be brave and stealthy to snatch a patient out from under her care.

But in daily life she is a source of constant surprise.

Yesterday I was mixing apple cake with my hands, which is the only way to mix my kind of apple cake. She came to the door of the kitchen and said, "I want to pay you now so I won't have to bother you later on." It was the worst possible time, but I forsook the cake and took her money.

I love to play bridge with her, whether as partner or opponent. She has the unique habit of counting her points out loud. It gives us all a sense of security. We know just what to expect from her.

She nursed Clark Gable through his fatal illness, and she almost saved him. He told her if he recovered he would put her in the movies because she looked like Agnes Moore-head.

Her proudest triumph was teaching a woman in an iron lung to play chess. What a blessed service!

"I play a fairly good game of chess," she said modestly. "I used to play with the best chess player in California. He won every time. He wanted to marry me, but I wouldn't marry a man and go through life being beaten at chess."

It Makes a Difference

I PROFESS to be a religious woman but I abominate the frauds that have disgraced true religion. The cruelest fraud of all was the invention of eternal hell.

It is a wonder that Christianity has survived its traducers. As Dean Jewett said, "Young man, you must believe in God in spite of what the clergymen tell you."

Of course, no one really believes in eternal hell-fire. The human mind is not capable of grasping eternity. We can think of nothing that is without end. No God is so monstrous as to sentence men to such everlasting misery.

I once knew a gentle little woman who belonged to an old-fashioned church that still clung to a literal hell. Her husband was an inactive atheist. He died without salvation, according to her beliefs.

One day her daughter found her on the porch sitting quietly in her rocking chair, enjoying the sunset.

"Mother," her daughter said, "you do not believe in Hell. You could not sit here enjoying the sunset if you really thought father was burning in Hell."

The mother hesitated and then replied, "Well, I have changed my mind a bit since I have someone there."

Perfection

THE SEARCH for perfection is seldom rewarding. A man may have the perfect secretary and a woman a perfect cook, but no man has a perfect wife and no woman has found the perfect church, and the hope of finding one shadows the pleasure of the wife or church they already have.

I am never interested in a man's third wife, and this is usually true of the man himself. The pursuit is more exciting than the pursued.

And so it is with changing churches. Better to stay as close as you can to the one you were born in. The trouble is that every church teaches something that no thinking man can believe. No man but has his private doubts. They say that china eggs are just as effective as real eggs to make hens lay. No religion is so false that it does not find devoted disciples.

Contentment in part is putting up with what you have whether a husband, a wife, or a church. It may be that we are looking for the wrong things. No wife can make a toneless man to sing and a church cannot give you salvation. A husband or wife is only someone to share your work, your grief, your humiliation or good fortune. And churches should help us live in peace with each other. Going to heaven is only a side issue.

I once heard a Doctor of Divinity preach a sermon—a sermon I shall never forget. He was a kindly, eloquent man with a soft voice, but what he said was harsh and cruel. The doctor said that getting to Heaven was like spelling the unabridged dictionary from cover to cover without missing a single word. If you misspelled one word you were out.

I had just finished working my way through college. It had been a hard four years and I was tired. I decided then and there not to try working my way to Heaven which appeared to be even more difficult.

Of course, the ministerial committee met with the doctor and told him never to preach that sermon again. In the end the man went to the insane asylum.

The search for perfection leads into strange paths where it may be impossible to turn back.

Better to Give Than to Receive

I WONDERED why he was so much happier this Christmas. He and his wife always visit us sometime during the holidays. He is principal of a high school, and I suspect he is one of those principals who dislike children. His wife is a blithe spirit. Even if you locked her in a closet she would give a party.

She had two children when she married the high school principal. In my opinion he was not a good stepfather—no physical abuse but too much criticism and not enough praise. I once suggested that the younger boy would be better off on the ranch, but it did not seem possible. It would have injured his pride—proof of the fact that we did not think he was qualified for the part of stepfather.

Time has passed; the older son has graduated from college and the younger boy, Elliot, is on his way through high school. I tried all these years to ignore their problem, enjoy the wife and forget the husband. I find it easy to pretend that some people do not exist.

This year all was changed. The principal of the high school was the life of the party.

"What has happened?" I whispered to the wife. I could not wait to be alone with her.

She smiled and leaned closer to me. "He bought Elliot a new car for Christmas. I don't know which one is the happiest, Elliot or my husband."

Hard to Understand

MY PASTOR told me this story. A daughter confided to her parents that she was going to have a child. She and the child's father, who is blind, were in college in their junior year. There was consternation in both families. The boy's father lived in a country where abortion was legal, and he volunteered to take the girl into his home and arrange to send her to a reputable clinic.

He and his wife treated the girl with great kindness. They introduced her to their friends. They took her sightseeing. They visited her at the hospital and sent her flowers.

The girl returned to college, and immediately both the father and the mother wrote the son uncompromising letters telling him never to mention the girl's name, and never to bring her into their home. They threatened to cut off his allowance and disinherit him if he married the girl.

What are the boy and girl to do now? They are in love.

To Tell the Truth

THERE ARE various standards for telling the truth. How much should be told and how much withheld? How far can one tell the technical truth and still deceive the public without its becoming a moral issue?

Some time ago I was introduced to a woman who had the same name as a famous actress. The name was hers rightfully, but she wanted the neighbors to believe that she was the famous actress and had gone into seclusion. I had met the great lady in her day and I knew that she had adopted a daughter and named her Constance after a friend of mine. Finally I tired of pretending I was deceived, so I said to her, "What ever became of Constance?"

The poor woman looked bewildered and replied, "It's been so long ago I can't remember." The glamour faded. I think the woman was relieved. She must have tired of the effort to maintain the reputation of another woman who was a stranger to her.

Recently I was asked to write an interview endorsing a measure on the June ballot. I am inclined to exaggerate, within limits, for a good cause. My son said the interview contained one statement that was not strictly true. I reconsidered and inserted the word "hardly" which satisfied him.

The incident reminded me of Great Uncle John. When he left the farm he held an old-fashioned auction and sold everything except a few pieces of furniture.

Uncle John had practically made a profession of telling the truth. His friends and neighbors measured the truth by his standards.

He had a Jersey cow which was an exceptionally good cow, but she was nervous, like all Jersey cows. She had the habit of lifting her leg while she was being milked. She had never kicked anyone or anything. True to his principles, when the Jersey cow came up for sale, Uncle John insisted on announcing that while she never kicked she had the habit of lifting her hind leg.

The Jersey cow sold for five dollars. Uncle John was the one member of the family who never regretted the loss of the hundred dollars. His reward is that whenever a member of the family is tempted to overstep the truth he is reminded of Great Uncle John and the Jersey cow.

A Welcome Guest

FATHER CARTER is my favorite Episcopal priest. He has an endearing piety and leaves me with a brighter outlook on this life and a gleam of hope for the next. Elisha's "room on the wall" is always waiting for him.

When I stoutly refused to take money for his night's lodging he said I reminded him of Rosa Lewis. I am sure it was not because Rosa was mistress to King Edward the Seventh. She had other endearing qualities.

King Edward gave Rosa the Cavendish Hotel in return for her services. When Father Carter was a young man in London before the Second World War, he and his brother were frequent guests at the Cavendish. Rosa refused to take money for their dinners. No doubt she enjoyed their wit and gaiety, and besides the brother played the piano rather well.

One day the boys planned to take two girls to the theater and to the hotel for a late dinner. They wanted to make sure that they would be allowed to pay for the dinners, so Father Carter talked to Rosa beforehand and insisted that he would not consent to be her guest. Rosa agreed.

That night when he went to pay his bill Rosa looked embarrassed. "Oh, I am so sorry," she said. "I made a mistake and charged your bill to the customer who just left."

Rosa is dead and now they have torn down the Cavendish Hotel. I grieve for them both.

A Last Sunrise Service

TOMORROW IS Easter morning but there will be no sunrise service on the ranch. The small children will hunt eggs and the breakfast tables will be decorated with tulips and gardenias. The smell of gardenias always reminds me of Easter morning.

Mrs. Murray, who owned the guest ranch across the

river, invited us each year to a sunrise service at her home. She had a high knoll which was just the place to welcome the dawn.

I remember one year when members of the Hall Caine choir stood on the side of the hill and just as the first rays of the sun reached them they burst into "Roll the Stone Away."

No one will ever forget that morning. I stood between Leatrice Joy and Alma Ciannelli. There was absolute silence, not a whisper to shatter the spell that held us together.

After Mrs. Murray died I tried to duplicate those wonderful mornings. Never try to imitate a perfect memory. Let it lie where it falls, safe in the past.

I heard that there was a quartet at the air base close by, which was available for a small fee. They came to see me and I loaned them a station wagon to make sure they would be on time in the morning, and I invited friends and neighbors to join me at the ranch.

I learned later that the station wagon had been up all night going from club to club in an effort to spend the money I had paid in advance.

The quartet came over the hill only seconds in advance of the sun. They climbed to the balcony and greeted its first rays with "I Met My Mother at the Railway Station" in four parts.

A Final Farewell

YESTERDAY THE Court of Inquiry handed down what I was pleased to regard as a just verdict. A group of boys had defied the sergeant in the prison camp in San Francisco. They were charged with mutiny. The Court dismissed the charge and found them guilty of a minor offense. How could sitting quietly on a bench possibly constitute mutiny?

When the Second World War broke out and my two sons enlisted I registered for a course in military law. Little good it did them or me. Under no circumstances would they allow me to interfere on their behalf. I never understood their attitude. As boys they had not been easily subdued. In the end they both earned commissions. That may be the answer.

When my younger son, nineteen, was commissioned he explained it by saying that they made him an officer just to punish two other fellows.

Although I was of no service to my own sons I did my bit during the war. I continued to exploit my knowledge of military law whenever I found an audience or a suitable occasion.

Our home was and is only ten miles from a large army air field, and during the war many officers took advantage of our hospitality and lived on the ranch until they went into combat. My close association with these officers made our victory seem incredible. Of course, this was just after war was declared and they were a motley lot, promoted because they had been amateur radio operators, civilian pilots or expert mechanics. Authority ill became them. How we won the war with such men still astonishes me.

One man remained for nine weeks and gained my hearty contempt. He was ill-mannered and cruel, and but for the war I would not have kept him as a guest. At last to my relief he was ordered to North Africa.

His final act enraged me. He boasted at the dinner table that a corporal under his command asked for a few hours leave because his wife was having their first baby in the hospital in San Bernardino forty miles away. The major refused the request and the boy went anyway—brave boy.

The major told the story with great glee. "I broke him to a private and a private he will stay." That night I decided that he was a man who would not escape my vengeance. I could not wait for Providence to repay him.

The next morning I sent word that I was ill in my room and that I wanted to say goodbye. The major came willingly.

"Major," I began, "you have lived in my house for two months. I have never seen you when I thought you were entirely sober. You have never shown a kindness to anyone but your dog. You have been cruel to your wife. You have boasted of your cruelty to your men. You have been a most unpleasant guest and I am happy to see you go. I pity the men under you and I am glad that my sons are going to another theater. Goodbye."

The man was so shocked he could not say a word. He muttered and sputtered and fled down the hall and outside where the official car was waiting. There was no time to return.

He was heard to say as he entered the car, "That woman gave me the worst dressing down I ever heard in my life and, my God, I just stood there and took it."

He survived the war but never came back to the ranch.

Frustration

THE LAMP is back from the repair shop.

It was once a carriage lamp, now it stands beside the piano in the living room. One cupid is permanently disabled. It met with an accident when we had a group of counselors from a nearby college. They brought their children because, as they said, there was no way children could get into trouble on a ranch. As everyone knows, children can get into trouble anywhere on earth.

One of the boys, about four years old, started to climb the antique lamp. The mother was alarmed. She called to him across the room, "Wait, dear, until I can hold it for you." She was too late. The cupid was broken.

After the guests left I asked Jean why her children were different. "I never took child psychology," she replied, "so

I was never afraid of frustrating my children." Could it be that we are facing a generation of children who have missed the advantages of frustration?

Recognition

BEING SOMETHING of an exhibitionist myself, I can sympathize with those who are presently seeking personal significance. We are not the happy people.

When I observe the surge of the younger generation I think I see one of their prime objects as the desire to be recognized individually or in groups. Watch television. See the exhibition by young militants in front of the camera. And when the camera is turned on an audience there are always one or two in the room who hold up their hands and wave. Has television helped to solve our problems?

There are many ways of seeming important. Some of them do not serve their purpose. Conspicuous glasses do not make the wearer a Ph.D., nor does taking the best seat on the plane give one social standing. Long hair will not remind everyone of the first president of the United States, and it may well prevent a man from becoming president of his company. Read what happened to Absalom.

A Surprise Interview

IT WAS Aunt Nellie who taught me not to talk down to children or ask them silly questions. She said she learned her lesson one day as she was sitting on the balcony of a local department store. A stranger sat beside her nursing a baby.

My aunt, who loved babies, smiled at the child and asked, "Is it good?"

She was startled when the child looked up at her and said, "Sure," and turned back to his dinner.

Ask a Boy

I AM happily surprised at the skill of this younger generation twice removed from mine. There are frequent occasions when I am grateful for their advice.

Last Monday I had trouble with my car. It left me stranded with a load of vegetables next to the market. I sent for the man from the garage. The next day, Tuesday, I was assured that it was ready for the road. It took me as far as the polling place, where I voted Republican, and there it remained. Again the mechanic came for it. He said it needed a new battery. The battery was only eighteen months old and should have been good for at least six months longer.

When I came home I consulted Scott, my fourteen-year-old grandson. I have great respect for his opinion of cars. His attitude toward cars reminds me of an evangelist. He thinks no car is beyond redemption. One of his favorite cars is an old truck named Flint. I think it once served a term in the army. Scott became so attached to Flint that the neighbor gave it to him, pink slip and all. The other day he asked me for a roll of pink toilet paper. I said I had only yellow paper, so he decided that would do. Now Flint runs with a roll of yellow toilet paper instead of an oil filter.

I called the garage and insisted that they listen carefully to what Scott had to say about my car. He assured me that it was not the battery and he told me why. He said it was either one of two things—I've forgotten what they were. The mechanic at the garage promised to heed Scott's advice.

When I called for my car I asked, "Was it the battery?"

"No."

"What is the charge?"

"Nothing."

I said no more. I drove away silently.

I am told that when Daniel escaped from the lions' den he never went back for his hat.

Something Is Wrong with the Colleges

SOMEONE AT the breakfast table this morning asked me if I thought a college education was necessary for success. Certainly not. Furthermore, I do not think financial success is a prime reason for going to college. I wanted my children to have a college education for other reasons—first, to enjoy the companionship of educated people and to be enjoyed by them; second, to develop their latent talents for self-expression; and finally, to enjoy the days of their youth. My college days were the happiest days of my life. Colleges no longer offer these advantages.

Alas, it is true that half of those who die while going to college are suicides. Something is wrong—tragically wrong. I wish I knew the answer. I do have some suggestions.

Sitting at the same breakfast table was a man who is a well-known professor from Cal Tech. He remarked that he had the qualifications to teach in any university in the United States, but that he could not teach in any high school in California. We have a second generation of professors who are undereducated and overpaid, banked by tenure. They have specialized in such subjects as the kind of furniture for a third-grade class, in the reaction of the community to the football team, in the graffiti in the public toilets, and these are the subjects they are prepared to teach— not the academic subjects that delighted my generation. And because they are themselves ignorant of the humanities, they join in and stimulate campus rebellions. They are pursued by fears for their own safety.

Help is at hand—the inexorable theory of the pendulum is working. The last session of the legislature reduced the number of required units in education from twenty-two to nine. Which means that future teachers will have the opportunity to study the subjects which they intend to teach.

Incompetent instructors invariably make the most outrageous assignments. My granddaughter graduated from Pomona College a year ago. She showed me the books she was supposed to read to prepare for comprehensives. The task was humanly impossible. Some of her classmates came to the ranch to study. They were all on the verge of nervous breakdowns—taking pills to keep them awake, taking pills to go to sleep.

Came the final two days which were to decide who would graduate. The first day some of the class became ill, some left the room. The others did the best they could.

The next morning the monitor announced that half of the tests from the previous day had been destroyed. The papers had not even been corrected. The examination had been written by a professor who was away on sabbatical and did not relate to the assignments the class had been given.

Where was the head of the English Department when the examination was given? Probably in his ivory tower writing a book. And that too is a detriment to our colleges. The slogan "Publish or perish" has done them grave harm. Governor Reagan, among other wise men, has denounced it. These men and women would do well to give more attention to teaching and wait until they retire to write books.

Examinations

EXAMINATIONS ARE not an accurate measure of knowledge. Some students are never at their ease when too much depends on an examination. They seldom do their best.

When my children were in high school the principal gave a short course in how to take an examination. It helped them all through college. There is an art to taking an examination which should be taught in every high school.

When I was a student in Andrews University I was obliged to take an examination on the history of music, for which I was unprepared. The history of music gives a wide scope for imagination. The next day I met the professor on her way to the library. "I know you are wrong," she said, not too kindly, "but it is going to take me all afternoon to prove it."

Advice to Teachers

I HAD trouble during my last year in Los Angeles Normal School which is now UCLA. I was teaching a practice class —the second grade. My supervisor was Mrs. Sector. She had one distinction—she was never forgotten. I have asked several graduates of my time. They have forgotten the names and faces of most of the faculty, but they all remember Mrs. Sector. Mrs. Sector and I disagreed on how to teach a second-grade class. For one thing she disapproved of laughter unless a definite period was set aside for it. I have felt the same disapproval in the courtroom.

I went to the superintendent of the training school and told her about my problem. She assured me that I would graduate. She said rather sadly that Mrs. Sector had no sense of humor and was to be pitied.

"You will be a good teacher," she continued, "but you will never progress much beyond the classroom." How right she was! "The children will like you but not the supervisors. You will never be principal of a school." Then she quoted Kipling to the effect that everyone should paint the things as he sees them for the God of things as they are.

The year I graduated from college Mrs. Sector went to Hawaii. When the Japanese bombed Pearl Harbor I thought of her, but I was not concerned for her safety.

After I had been practicing law for some time I was asked to address the assembly at the college. Dr. Millspaugh was still president. Here was my opportunity. I would retaliate. I told how I had nearly failed in my last year because of an inept supervisor. I said I had left the profession because I did not take kindly to increasing supervision.

I said that in my opinion teachers were taught to be overly dedicated. It was too much like taking the veil. The best teacher I ever knew never hesitated to call her principal and tell him to get a substitute. She had an important date for that day. It annoyed her principal but he was helpless because of her excellent record.

I quoted Rebecca of Sunnybrook Farm:

If joy and duty clash
Let duty go to smash.

I said that no teacher should submit to injustice or incompetence for fear of losing her job. Every teacher should be able to make a living outside of the schoolroom and be unafraid to try. I finished by saying that no one who was afraid of the children, afraid of the parents or the principal or the superintendent, or afraid of the school board should waste the best years of her life teaching school. Teachers were born not just to teach but to enjoy life.

I expected only silent disapproval. I was puzzled by the applause.

Then Dr. Millspaugh rose and said, "Mrs. Campbell, if

you will have that speech printed I will personally buy a thousand copies."

My revenge had misfired.

Benefits of Disaster

TWICE WITHIN two weeks Southern California has been declared a disaster area. Once should have been enough since one disaster ran concurrently with the other. First came the floods. It is sad that we can no longer enjoy "the slow rain tired of falling." The people who build on the sides of the mountains are always involved in one disaster or another— first comes the fire and then the flood. If they must live on a hillside, they should be content with a sod or a log house not so easily destroyed. For years the hillsides look dry and safe and people build enormously expensive houses, and then comes trouble and half their life's savings are swept away. Never build in canyons or on terraced land.

The second disaster followed close on the flood. An oil well broke away from the drillers. It was in the ocean about three miles offshore from beautiful Santa Barbara. The oil emptied into the ocean at the rate of twenty-one thousand gallons a day. I wonder how they could possibly measure that amount. The owners of the well worked frantically to repair the leak, but before they succeeded the oil had covered eighty square miles of the ocean and many miles of beach. I had pity for the people who lived along the shore and for the oil company who had the accident. They did everything possible to repair the damage, even to organizing rescue work for the water birds and establishing clinics to save them.

Birds are like their featherless friends. The wise ones escaped. I watched on television and saw only grebes, loons, and cormorants being bathed in solvent. Apparently the gulls, the ducks, the brants, the turnstones, the sandpipers, and the little sanderlings kept out of the oil slick.

And I saw one strange result of the accident. There were the long-haired hippies of whom I so fervently disapprove tenderly nursing the sick birds back to life. It takes such emergencies to bring out the best in men and women.

I was reminded of the poet who saw a swan struggling in the thick oil in the Arno River during the terrible Florence flood. It was helpless to free itself. Finally the poet phoned the police and the police ignored city-wide destruction and sent a rescue squad to save the swan.

It was said of Madame de Staël that she was so fond of helping people that she would push them in the water just for the pleasure of rescuing them.

We have a neighbor with whom we seldom communicate, but let the house catch fire or let a horse break a leg, and he rejoices to be on hand to help.

I had a friend who was working for the Red Cross when Mount Pelée erupted on Martinique. I saw his wife shortly after it happened and asked about her husband. She replied, "Oh, he has gone to Martinique. No disaster is complete until Jack gets there."

The Great Depression

It is more than forty years since the beginning of the Great Depression. Books are being written about those days. I hope the writers will remember that very soon after 1929 the government met the challenge and silenced its critics.

Victorville was then a village of about three thousand people, the majority of whom were dependent on two cement companies—the Riverside and the Oro Grande. Both companies kept one man in every family employed in spite of the fact that they operated at a loss for many, many months. No one in our town referred to them as soulless corporations.

We had acres and acres planted to alfalfa that year. The price of alfalfa fell from $25 to $9 a ton. Our tenant farmers were under a lease which provided a penalty for nonpayment of rent. Mr. Campbell could have taken all the valuable machinery they owned. Instead he allowed them to move away and take the money for the alfalfa and their equipment with them.

One of the wives later boasted that they had outwitted

Mr. Campbell. It was not only ungrateful but untrue. No one ever outwitted Kemper Campbell.

When times were difficult few exacted the ultimate dollar, and those who were able employed as many people as they could afford. Men learned the meaning of the Golden Rule.

No Need to Worry

ALMOST EVERYONE is kind to old people. It is one of the compensations for the loss of one's youth.

My cousin who is old but not nearly as old as I am trades with a grocery clerk who is old but not as old as she is. He calls her "my love." The other day she bought a small bottle of candied ginger which cost almost a dollar. The clerk looked alarmed. "My love," he asked, "can you afford that?" My cousin assured him that she really could afford the ginger, and to prove it she opened the bottle then and there and they sat down together and ate it all.

Touché

SOMETIME IN June of 1969 I received a letter from a woman in Connecticut. She was a stranger to me. I had never heard of her, and she did not say why she had chosen to appeal to me for help.

She begged me to stop the plans for landing on the moon. She said the moon was God's hideaway and that terrible things would happen if man invaded His privacy.

My reply was brief. "You simply can't be serious."

I did not hear from her again until the middle of September. By then the stock market was going down, hopes of a negotiated peace were fading, and earthquakes and tornadoes were reported in the daily papers.

Her reply was as brief as mine had been. She wrote, "I told you so," and signed her name.

A Stranger at the Gate

COMMUNISM WAS not popular during the Great Depression. The right to free speech applies to Communists as well as to Republicans, but it does not guarantee them the right to use a dinner table as a forum. They make unpleasant guests.

There was Mrs. V. She came for a week. She painted a dark picture of circumstances as she found them. She said that fifty babies had died of starvation in Bakersfield. Why Bakersfield—a modest town surrounded by fertile fields and oil wells which continued to pump oil all through the Depression.

My fourteen-year-old son asked if they buried them all in the same grave. Mrs. V. did not reply.

"I cannot speak for all America," I said, "but as far as I know there is no one in California either hungry or cold. I am no better than my friends and neighbors, but not one of us would turn a hungry person away."

Then she told about a group of young people in Los Angeles who were hungry, and I said that I might not be able to take the whole group, but that I could give some of them work on the ranch.

Her answer surprised me. "These people are in love with the dance. They would rather starve than give up their art." I withdrew my offer.

Some weeks later a young man came to our city office. He said he was hungry and had no home. He had a soft English accent that never fails to appeal to me. He professed to be an entertainer and he slipped behind the door and came out as Harry Lauder or Bert Lahr or Ed Wynn or some other famous person. I told him I did not entertain my guests—they entertained me—and I suggested that he try Palm Springs. I gave him enough money to buy food and a ticket to Palm Springs.

The next weekend I found him at the ranch. He had

failed in Palm Springs. He did look too thin, and I told him I would weigh him in and weigh him out, and he could stay until he had gained fifteen pounds. I suggested ways by which he could earn his board and room and spending money. He had only one suit, so I loaned him one of Mr. Campbell's suits and sent his suit to the cleaner.

The following weekend I found that he was unwilling to do odd jobs but instead he was engaged in telling fortunes for a fee and borrowing money and cigarettes from the guests. He was in business for himself.

He boasted of having many friends in Oxford, and he named Sir Thomas Wood as one of them. I suggested that he go back to England and seek help from these friends.

"Oh, I could never do that," he exclaimed in horror. "You see my mother was a Russian refugee. She went back to Russia as a spy and her friends betrayed her. She is now in Siberia. I could never go back." Well, there was no way of disproving his story.

After three weeks I decided I had to protect my guests. He was leaning too heavily on their generosity. I told him he must give me references. He named several prominent people in the theater, but it happened they were all in New York or Europe. Finally he mentioned Hal Roach and my Communist guest, Mrs. V. I called Hal Roach Studios. They had never heard of him.

The plot unfolded. Mrs. V. had sent him. I had left my door wide open.

When I returned to the ranch he had gone. I was relieved, although he left in Mr. Campbell's suit.

I had met the test. No hungry man had been turned away from my door. I am sure he gained more than fifteen pounds.

A Great Woman

LAST NIGHT at dinner I sat beside a justice of the Supreme Court. Quite unexpectedly he asked me if I had ever met Eleanor Roosevelt. I had never met Mrs. Roosevelt, but the question reminded me of that great woman and all that she accomplished in a lifetime shorter than mine. Although I am a devout Republican I can still see and appreciate the light that shines from kind deeds that bear her name. She could and did pass miracles.

Of these miracles I have two recollections. I live in a village near an airfield. During the Second World War we were hard put to house the families of the airmen whose last assignment was Victorville before being sent overseas. Marion Stallsmith found dozens of trailers less than a hundred miles away. The army refused to move them. They were being kept for an emergency which never happened. The expected emergency seldom does. Marion wrote directly to Eleanor. Within two weeks the army was ordered to move the trailers at once.

And again during the war I became alarmed at the conduct of the Dairymen's Association in California. They were taking advantage of temporary wartime regulations to put the small dairymen out of business. I knew this because besides practicing law, I was raising dairy cows, and I frequently bought calves from small dairies.

I went to the office of the association. No one asked me inside the rail or offered me a chair. The executive in charge refused to see me.

I wrote to Eleanor Roosevelt. In a few days this same man called me for an appointment. I replied and I quote, "I do not need to see you. I have nothing to discuss. You have had your orders and now there is no problem."

How did she do it? How could one person be omnipresent—be everywhere, see everything? And she taught us the value of silence. She never answered Drew Pearson. How it frustrated him.

Silence is the one defense that is not subject to cross-examination and calls for no rebuttal.

Happy Vagabonds

MONDAY MY daughter and her husband returned from a ten-week trip to Europe. They traveled in a van with two musicians and their son and daughter. They report that the trip was perfect—not a single disappointment or unhappy encounter. It is refreshing to hear their glowing account of how strangers welcomed them and friends made them feel at home. Money for the trip was well spent for lasting happiness.

Now that a trip to Europe is within the reach of people of modest means many of our friends are returning eager to tell of their adventures. Those who enjoyed Europe or any other part of the globe are listened to with great interest, but travelers who return with complaint after complaint are "crashing bores." I do not want to hear that the Egyptians hate us, that the French rob us, and the English are ungrateful. I have never found this to be true.

These critical people would be wise to spend their time shelling peas in their own backyards. As Emerson said, "No man ever went to Europe an ass and came back a horse."

Minor misfortunes can spoil an entire trip.

My cousin went to Europe last August. She checked her suitcase at the Los Angeles airport. She was gone a month and the poor suitcase never did catch up with her. It followed her all over Europe. Fortunately she wore a durable suit when she boarded the plane. I never tire of hearing her tell about her wonderful trip. The lost suitcase made it even more memorable.

It doesn't take an earthquake or pestilence to ruin a trip for some people. A traffic ticket, a missing suitcase, a day's delay, a crowded train—and all is lost.

Once when Joe was about four years old his aunt took him to a moving picture show. All through the show he kept moving about and saying, "We won't let it spoil our good times, will we?"

When he came home I found that a misplaced safety pin

had been sticking into the poor boy the whole time. Joe's advice has been added to the store of family wisdom. It has often helped us to meet bad luck halfway. "We won't let it spoil our good times, will we?"

Stupidity

THIS MORNING at the breakfast table the doctor and I talked about the problem of helping people who are too poor to help themselves. I told the doctor that I envied him. Doctors can do some permanent good. If a poor man has malaria and the doctor cures him he may not have malaria again. This is not true for lawyers. If we help a poor and stupid man to collect ten thousand dollars he will be back in eleven months penniless. He is no better off. In fact he is worse off. He has tasted money—bought a new car, a new television set, and had a good time at the races.

We were not talking about ignorance. There is help for the ignorant—those who don't read Shakespeare because the print is too fine. But they often do well, for there are many tasks for ignorant but skillful people to perform. The man who asks, "What was Waterloo?" or "Who wrote the first dictionary?" may be a welcome mechanic.

I dread hiring stupid men, both for their sakes and mine. Once we had such a man working for us. One day when he was off duty he tried to show a fellow worker how to run the alfalfa grinder—tried to show him with his glove on. He lost three fingers of his right hand, leaving him with only his first finger and his thumb. Of course we were not liable. It was his day off and at no time was it his duty to instruct the other man, but we made no point of our liability. The Industrial Accident Commission awarded him a small monthly pension for life.

We continued to hire him with disastrous results. He married the cook. She persuaded him to apply for a lump sum. I begged him to take the life pension, small as it was, but the cook won. He insisted that he didn't miss the three fingers. In fact he said that he found out that the three fingers had really been in his way. In less than a year the cook and the seven thousand dollars disappeared.

There was a touching series of pictures on television not long ago. I remember one picture of a woman from Texas who was greatly overweight. Her complaint was that she had to eat meat and potatoes because she could not afford vegetables.

During the Second World War fresh vegetables were scarce on the desert. My aunt from Illinois came to my rescue. She showed me plenty of edible vegetables on the ranch. There was sour dock and lamb's quarters and mushrooms. Watercress grew along a tiny stream, and milkweed grew everywhere. And she told me that the tiny new shoots of milkweed were almost as good as asparagus. And there is a plant that thrives every spring that improves any salad. I forget what it is from year to year and have to go about tasting bitter weeds until I find it. When tea is scarce we have Ephedra which grows on the ranch and is very wholesome.

I am sure there are more vegetables growing wild in Texas than grow in our semi-desert area, and the search for them would have been beneficial exercise for the woman who was overweight. Poverty is not the main cause of hunger in America. I have eaten many a delicious meal at the table of poor people. It is stupidity that causes suffering and malnutrition.

Johnny

JOHNNY IS gone. He left yesterday. His father was the best milker we ever had. He followed the cows to Fresno and Johnny followed his father.

Johnny's father loved cows and his mother loved herself, but as far as I know no one loved Johnny.

Johnny lived on the ranch for seven years, and I don't think we did him one bit of good. He was a strange child and the only child of his kind that I ever liked. He never had the vaguest notion about the meaning of truth or private property. He was our lost and found department. If we lost a beach towel or a tennis racket or left a purse by the pool we had only to ask Johnny. He would look wide-eyed and return the article.

His mother was careful about one thing. She cautioned him not to pick the strawberries until they were ripe and not to knock the peaches off the trees until they were ready to eat. We tried to persuade him to leave the fruit alone, but he and the birds together usually shared the crop.

We gave him permission to let his visiting cousins swim in the pool with him. After that all the children wandering by became his "cousins." He loved the pool. For him it had two uses—to swim in and to throw stones in. When we warned him that if he continued to throw stones and broken glass into the pool he could no longer swim in it, his eyes filled with tears and he promised faithfully never to do it again, but he never emptied his pockets—just waited until no one was watching him.

I finally persuaded him that people would rather see their flowers growing in the garden than have him pick them and present them as a ragged bouquet. He was hungry for praise.

As he grew older he developed a good business sense. He would sell whatever he thought we no longer needed. One day he sold a minibike that the children had outgrown. It was a bargain at a dollar. Just as the purchaser was loading the bike onto a truck the owner happened by.

He never had anything of his own except a bicycle. I was so happy when he came riding by on a white pony, but it turned out that the pony was ill and had to be destroyed.

The principal of his school wanted him to attend summer school. He was lagging behind his class. She offered to send the school bus to pick him up, but his mother refused to let him go. He was an only child and he had to wash the dishes. In the world where Johnny lived only children washed the dishes.

His prize possession was a picture of his mother in a compromising position. He was too young to know the value of blackmail.

I became really alarmed when he broke into a tenant's house and stole her transistor radio. The door was open but he preferred the window. He rode around the ranch on his bicycle the rest of the afternoon with the radio sounding off full blast. He was never secretive about his offenses. He admitted the theft, returned the radio, and his father fixed the window.

I asked my grandson if he couldn't talk to him about such conduct. He replied, "We have a lot in common, but we never discuss theft. It embarrasses us both."

Why did I like Johnny? Because he was the most grateful child I ever knew. What a precious virtue gratitude is! If we did Johnny the smallest favor his eyes filled with tears. Give him the simplest thing, compliment him on how well he swam, invite him to a hayride or let him ride one of our horses and his gratitude was almost more than I could bear. That is why I am so sad. We could do him no lasting good. The undercurrent was too strong—it was sweeping him away from us forever.

He did me one favor that I shall never forget. Someone unknown to me had planted marijuana on the ranch. The plants were just nicely above the ground when Johnny pulled them up, every one. He said he was looking for a four-leaf clover.

Johnny, dear, I hope some day you will find a whole field of four-leaf clovers.

Out of the Marsh

WHEN I am about to give up hope for the whole human race something usually happens to renew my faith and give me courage.

Pearl worked for us years ago. She was a beautiful girl. Her family were all dark-haired with black eyes, but she was blond and blue-eyed. Her family were proud of her although she was an illegitimate child begotten of some wanderer who passed on and was heard from no more.

When Pearl came to us she was the mother of an illegitimate child. She was not married and her mother took care of the child. Pearl was a quiet girl. We had no reason to find any fault with her except on one occasion when an actor took her to Arrowhead for the weekend. Even then I chose to blame the man.

Finally Pearl married a good man and her daughter Essie came to work for us. By that time having illegitimate children had become a family tradition. When it came Essie's turn she left us. That was three illegitimate children in a row—one in each generation.

By this time I had lost hope, interest, and even curiosity.

Years passed—Essie married and her husband adopted the child.

This June I attended a graduation exercise in my grandson's school, and there I saw Essie's child. She was not only beautiful like her grandmother, but she stood at the head of the class. She played her part very well—thanking all the teachers for their kindness and presenting them with a gift.

One could not tell which was the prouder parent—her mother or her stepfather.

I came home full of cheer. As my mother was fond of saying, "Out of the marsh the lily grows."

If the Wind Changes

I SAW a sad picture on television last night. A man and his wife were standing outside their modest home in Huntington Beach. I can remember when it was possible for poor people to buy a lot in Huntington Beach and enjoy the ocean as only the wealthiest can do today.

The man and his wife built their home many years ago. They had raised four children in this house. It looked comfortable—more spacious than the house we first owned in California.

The City of Huntington Beach has ordered the house torn down. Why? For one reason: there is a door between the kitchen and the bathroom. I am sure the door is kept closed. What happens to people who have a door between the kitchen and the bathroom? Do they contract measles or whooping cough, or cancer, or heart trouble?

The man's comment broke my heart. "I will never own another home," he said. "I have retired and I have no money to build again."

The inspectors say that the improvement is demanded by the people. Can it be that they are standing with one foot on the rail and imagine they are listening to the voice of the people?

Not long ago I spoke at a service club. I am at war with Urban Renewal. I said that a man went to his doctor. The doctor told the man he had diabetes. The man asked the doctor why and the doctor replied, "It is because the studs in your house are only three-fourths of an inch thick instead of seven-eighths as the law requires. You must bring your house up to standard."

One man in the audience took me seriously and had his house inspected.

What has become of that constitution that protected a man and his property? Legalized injustice against which a man has no defense is more dangerous than communism.

They say that Nero only intended to burn the slums but the wind changed and instead the fire destroyed the finest houses in Rome. It could happen again.

A Common Complaint

WHENEVER I return from a visit to a city, an island, or a National Park, someone says, "You should have seen the place before there were so many people there. I enjoyed it then." I feel sorry for these men and women for they will probably never have the world to themselves again.

I suppose New York was different before the Dutch came and disturbed the Indians, and it has been changing ever since. Still I love New York. The busy people interest me and I hasten to keep up with them. The skyline thrills me. I rejoice in the courtesy of the hotel clerks, the waiters, and especially the taxi drivers.

Three years ago when I returned from my first visit to Hawaii, my friends looked at me with pity. I should have seen Hawaii before the tourists came. In a few years they will be saying the same thing about Tahiti and Moorea.

Catalina is a beautiful island. "But have you seen all those boats in the harbor?" A harbor full of boats in the sunset is a beautiful sight to see.

There are too many people looking over the rim of the Grand Canyon, too many people crowding into Yosemite Valley—as though a million eyes could diminish the grandeur of Half Dome.

It was ever so. I have no doubt the citizens of Cairo looked with apprehension at the building of the Pyramids. Egypt was never the same again.

Let us enjoy the world as it is and then leave it much as we find it.

Poor Isaiah

I HAVE just finished reading the most astonishing book— *The Territorial Imperative.* It convinced me that what I have long suspected is true. All people and all animals have one desire—to leave things as they are.

When my boys went to the war they cautioned me, "Don't change anything while we are gone. Don't even let them put down cement sidewalks. Leave everything alone until we come home." They wanted to picture it just as it was when they left.

Guests return to the ranch, some of them after as long as thirty years, and the first thing they say is, "It is so wonderful to find it exactly as we remember it."

When friends ask me to identify birds they have seen in their walks across the ranch, I ask them where they saw the bird and whether it was in a tree, perched on the fence or on the ground. That helps me to answer their questions, for birds return to the same place year after year.

This spring we offered the Boy Scouts a hundred dollars if they would spend Saturday cleaning up the ranch. We live on the edge of a vast desert so the results of their efforts were limited, but they did clear the rabbit bush out of a neglected patio.

About noon one of the guests called me to see the excitement in this same patio. A roadrunner was causing a great commotion. He was angry to the point where he looked twice his size. Every feather was standing straight up and out. He walked around the patio. He jumped to the wall. He jumped down into the patio and then back on the wall. He is usually a quiet bird, but he was making the most raucous sounds. I have seen a similar performance in a corner of Hyde Park.

Then I remembered that it was here the roadrunner had built his nest for many summers. He was back to survey his land and inventory the building materials available, only to find that all the shade and protection were gone. The roadrunner has my sympathy.

Civilization is boxing us in. Isaiah complained more than 2,000 years ago: "Woe unto them that join house to house, that lay field to field, till there be no place that they may be placed alone in the midst of the earth!"

Desolation

SMOKE IS billowing up on the ranch along the river. We owned that ranch until 1932 when we sold it to an excellent farmer.

For half a century there was a beautiful orchard of Bartlett and Winter Nelis pears that never failed to bear an abundant crop each fall—enough for all the neighbors. Now the orchard has been uprooted and the trees burned. Not even the precious fruit wood was saved.

And today they are destroying cottonwood lane which has been a landmark on this desert for more than fifty years. How can they bear to destroy these benevolent trees that have saved the lives of many weary travelers? Have they counted how long it takes to grow a tree that can be seen on the horizon for miles and miles and promises water for man and beast?

These men have even invaded the mesa and are leveling the Joshua trees which were here before the Indians came. One of my friends protested and the offender said, "Oh, we will replant them." Replant a Joshua tree—as simple as bringing back the dodo bird or the passenger pigeon.

Who are these people who drive the monstrous tractors bringing swift destruction? They are the famous company who are planning a community of thirty-eight hundred homes where there are two farmhouses today. There will be a manmade lake, a golf course, and a great shopping center where our cattle once grazed and our horses rested after a day's work.

But why, oh, why did they sacrifice the pear orchard, cottonwood lane and the Joshua trees? Wise men would have included them in their elaborate plans. Men at their drawing boards in tall office buildings, men who have never seen our desert order their engineers to wreak havoc and do it quickly.

They do not know or care that our desert is different from all other deserts. It is covered by rabbit bush, creosote, ephedra, and honey mesquite. They do not know that these friendly bushes will never grow again. Russian thistle will take their places. The books call Russian thistle a "weed of disturbance," and scientists cannot explain why it will never grow where the ground has not been disturbed.

Next spring there will be three thousand acres of Russian thistle. It will roll in the wind for miles across the desert as far as my home and beyond, and we will be ever closer to a real desert like the Sahara and the Gobi. By then these subdividers will take their money and be gone.

I stood on the bluff and looked over the land which a few months ago was a rich meadow. There was not a shrub or a tree left. Even the walls of the bluff had been denuded of every living thing. "We will plant again." Not in my lifetime. I took my last look at the devastation. I rejoice that I cannot see it from where I live.

It delighted me to hear that the Supreme Court of the state of Washington has issued a permanent injunction against this same company. Someone is watching them.

As my grandson Craig said, "They are improving the world beyond repair."

A Wrong Without a Remedy

I AM not sure which causes me the most concern—the atom bomb or the motorcycles. Both inventions have changed my world.

The hill back of my home is crossed and recrossed by paths. There were once cow paths. Now they are worn by motorcycles. There is a difference. Cow paths form a pattern. They go back and forth, evenly spaced from one side of the hill to the other. Motorcycles make no such design. Cow paths follow the contour of the hill and prevent erosion. Motorcycle paths encourage erosion.

There is nothing I can do about this invasion of my property. Warning signs do no good. They only tend to make criminals out of these reckless riders. Otherwise they are not conscious of breaking the law.

I could have them arrested for crossing my property line but it would only crowd the courts and delay the trials of more important cases. I am helpless. It is a wrong without a remedy. I must learn to live and enjoy life within the sound of motorcycles. It is the penalty I pay for owning a stretch of hill and woods and lakes and pastures which tempts intruders.

I learned a lesson long ago from a really wonderful woman. Mr. and Mrs. Rindge came to California many, many years ago. They took a deep and unselfish interest in the little city of Los Angeles. Those were pioneer days and Mr. Rindge believed that Los Angeles would be a safer place to live if no liquor were sold to the Indians and outlaws. So for two years, he paid Los Angeles a sum equal to the amount of revenue it would have received from the sale of liquor.

Mr. and Mrs. Rindge became very wealthy. They owned the Santa Monica Mountains and miles of seashore. They had their own pier where seagoing vessels loaded and unloaded. I suppose their vast estate was almost as large as Rhode Island.

There was peace around them for many years, and then came the migration to California. Little by little the Santa Monica Mountains and the seashore were invaded. At first it was a minor problem.

After Mr. Rindge died, Mrs. Rindge, who was a righteous and law-abiding woman, tried to keep people off her property. She had the legal right to do so, but she was never successful. The harder she tried, the more problems she had.

She employed one of the best-known law firms in the city, the firm of Flint and McKay. I remember being in the courtroom one morning when a member of the firm rose and said, "I represent the Santa Monica Mountains." Everyone smiled. That was the secret of the conflict. No one could represent the Santa Monica Mountains. Ownership is qualified and can be enforced only by public opinion.

I once heard Clarence Darrow say, "Wasn't it wonderful of God to make so much fine oil for John D. Rockefeller?" His audience filled the Temple Auditorium. He paused; there was not a sound. We were all thinking our own thoughts.

God did not make the Santa Monica Mountains and miles of seashore for Mrs. Rindge alone; neither did He make this beautiful valley solely for me.

And so Mrs. Rindge lost her fight. There were ugly rumors of men with shotguns and, worse still, of broken glass strewn along the seashore where people went to bathe. Perhaps none of this was true.

Mrs. Rindge not only lost her fight for her rights, but worse still she lost her reputation for good will and natural dignity. I went to school with her son-in-law. He committed suicide. It is all a sad story with a sad ending.

I must learn to live with motorcycles and atom bombs. I shall content myself with the memory of the quiet days before either one was invented. Silence is one of our natural resources which is in grave danger of being lost forever.

Beware of Army Engineers

EVERYONE SAID it wouldn't work. There is an ancient water course that runs through the village of Victorville. It is called the Rio Grande Wash. In rare winters when we have heavy rainfall the water rushes down the Wash past two rows of houses across the ball park and down the main street. Even in the worst floods it does very little actual damage, but it is a threat to a part of the town. Someone (no one will admit to it today) suggested that the Rio Grande Wash would be a convenient way to spend government money.

The Army Engineers agreed and they drew up plans for a ditch about half as wide as the Panama Canal and deeper in places. The town was torn up all winter. You were never sure when you went in to shop which street would be open and which taken over by enormous equipment. At last the ditch was finished. It cost many times the value of the houses that were threatened.

Our local disaster director was pleased. He said he could direct almost everyone in the village to the ditch in case an atomic bomb was dropped on us. He said there would be room for all except a few undesirable people whom he had not planned to save anyway. Before we had the ditch we had to rely on an abandoned mine which would accommodate less than a thousand people.

It happened that this was a year for a flood—the worst

flood since 1938. Did the water go down the flood channel?
We watched anxiously, standing in the rain. Well, part of it
did and part of it ran past the houses and across the park as
usual. Not only that, but the river, which was a raging tor-
rent, ran up the new ditch to meet the incoming flood. It
was all confusion. Water has a will of its own and no one
can foretell which way it will go.

I wonder if the Army Engineers in Washington have
been told about what happened. They would surely be embarrassed. Noah must have been relieved when the Ark
floated.

The Corps of Army Engineers have a motto and their
motto is "We have the money. Why not?"

Not long ago the Engineers decided to destroy a beautiful avenue of trees in Marin County and replace it with a
cement ditch which served no useful purpose. My grandson
was one of the students who came from the College of
Marin to picket the Engineers. Some of the women of the
neighborhood chained themselves to the trees, but the Engineers went through with their plan, carting away both
the trees and the women.

The Corps of Army Engineers are indomitable. They
have never known defeat. If the President really wants to
win the war he should send them to Vietnam. Nothing can
stop them.

Election Issues

EVERY ELECTION year I am amazed at the issues that are raised by opposing candidates—issues over which the candidates have no control. They will accuse each other of being derelict in their duty when neither man has the legal authority to solve the problem.

. Local elections are often won by small margins. Yesterday I persuaded the help to vote for my favorite candidate for city council. Ten single votes were enough to elect him. I told the help that he was against the Vietnam War. I am sure this is true.

And why not? Big Bill Thompson was once elected mayor of Chicago because he took a firm stand against man-eating sharks and cyclones.

Cultivating Phobias

MOST OF the people I know have suffered from some unreasonable phobia. Some of these people are proud of their phobias and make excuses for them; others sincerely try to control them.

One of my sisters could not share a house with a mouse—not even a little field mouse who came in out of the cold.

Field mice are so superior to their city cousins. I had an aunt and now I have a granddaughter who finds it difficult to live in a world with spiders. The discovery of the violin-backed poisonous spider up from South America has not helped to quiet her fears. Some of my friends never come to the ranch, afraid of encountering a farm cat. I cannot understand their aversion to cats while they tolerate dogs who have the unpleasant habit of welcoming an acquaintance by trying to knock him down.

My daughter-in-law suffers from acrophobia. She was delighted to wake up the morning of the day she and her husband planned a trip up the Jungfrau—a deep fog enclosed the mountain so that she could see nothing from the train.

My obsession is claustrophobia. I will not enter an elevator alone. This is inconvenient. As I grow older and buildings grow higher it presents a problem.

I have tried to free myself from this handicap ever since an unfortunate experience on a trip to France. I was one of about two hundred guests invited to a luncheon in the Orangery at Versailles. I remember only the first course—a hard-boiled egg gazing up through a sphere of gelatin. It had a sinister look. I saw the massive closed doors and the barred windows. Fear possessed me. Did I expect all two hundred guests would be forgotten and left to mummify and be discovered by scholars a century later?

I am still embarrassed when I think of that luncheon and the panic that seized me. I must have been the strangest companion for the man beside me as I sat there glassy-eyed, eating nothing. The occasion was ruined for me and for him.

The memory of that awful day has helped me control my phobia. If the victim is ashamed of his phobia it becomes increasingly harmless.

My only defense is that the Orangery served as a political prison during the terrible days of the French Revolution. Did the soul of some poor victim take possession of me? If so it was useless. I do not communicate with the dead.

Status

I ATTENDED a women's club luncheon and listened to a lecture by a state officer on the status of women. I have never worried about our status. It depends almost entirely on where we are and what we are.

The speaker gave some interesting statistics. One-third of the working force in America are women. And happily three-fifths of the women who work are living at home with their husbands and families. I was glad to hear this.

The speaker tried to explain why women work. She had never worked she was proud to say, and she found it hard to understand those who did. She said one reason for working was that women were no longer compelled to have unwanted children. She gave this change her qualified approval. Then she said that families demanded more money today than they did twenty-five years ago. Certainly this is true.

Finally she conceded that some women worked for self-expression, for the joy of earning money, and for the rewards of accomplishment. I belonged to that class. I was a practicing attorney when I married Mr. Campbell. We wanted a family. I devoted nine years to the project, and then I returned to the office. My children were old enough to be cared for by others. No business was important enough to keep me away from them when they were sick or in trouble. Some of my happiest memories are of the times when they were recovering from illness and I could sit by their beds and enjoy them. We had long vacations together. Part of the time we communicated by long-distance telephone. The phones were always open and I welcomed a call from them. Help was available. They had the advantages that money could buy and today they enjoy a higher level of prosperity as a result of our joint efforts—Mr. Campbell's and mine.

And yet I have never dared to ask them whether they think I was wise in leaving them to the care of others. I do not know what their answer would be. Now that they are grown I realize how much of their childhood I missed. Oh well, there are the grandchildren.

I am often asked whether I think it is wise to work in your husband's office. My answer is emphatic. Yes, if he wants you there and if you are positive that he is more intelligent than you are. Never work in your husband's office if you feel superior to him. I had no such problem.

The almost thirty years that I worked in my husband's office were among the happiest years of my life. We never disagreed in the office—we reserved our arguments for the weekends.

If a woman wants to work she must forgo her prescribed right to recurring illness. This is a real sacrifice; women have so long made much of this advantage.

Recently I was asked to go with two other women to discuss the women's lounge in the new law building at U.S.C. The building is costing three million dollars, but there is such a demand for space that the lounge is only twenty by fourteen. We were told that eight feet were to be partitioned off and would contain three cots. We were outraged. Why destroy the beauty of the lounge to memorialize the fact that some women are neurotic? The University has a dispensary open to both men and women. We lost. The men would have it so.

When we were married I told my husband that if he was not too proud to let me work he did not need to take out life insurance. Life insurance is extremely expensive. I could not bear to think of his saving money which I could only enjoy if he died. That was our agreement.

Insurance agents buzzed around the office for years. They were appalled by our lack of foresight. One day one of the most persistent agents called. Finally Mr. Campbell said, "You might as well give up. I do not need life insurance. If I die Mrs. Campbell will take care of the children. Her office is next door to mine. If she dies I will provide for them."

That was a new argument. The agent was not prepared to meet it. He had reached the elevator when he turned and came back. He tapped Mr. Campbell on the shoulder. "Remember the change of life," he said.

I Remind Him of a Man Who Went to Heaven

WHEN HE first told me the story I had already heard it. It is never necessary to say, "I have heard that story before." It is much kinder to laugh and appear to enjoy the joke.

It was one of those stories about a man who went to Heaven and encountered Peter with disastrous results. I find this sort of story mildly amusing at best.

The second time he told me the story I refrained from reminding him that he had told me the same story before. I like the man.

The third time he told the story I was really amused. My laughter was steadfast. I knew the man was helpless. Every time he sees me he is reminded of this story, so I am prepared to hear it again and again. It is no longer trite. Each repetition only adds to my enjoyment.

Signs of Improvement

I HEARD Bishop Sheen on television the other night. He is gracious and benevolent. I was so pleased to have his final verdict on birth control.

David Frost would not desist—he compelled the Bishop to answer. To my great relief he finally said that birth control was not a mortal sin. I have lived to see a revolution gaining strength not outside but within the Church.

The interview reminded me of a ghastly evening a few years ago. I was asked to speak before the doctors of the valley. I must have been told that it was a staff meeting, but I ignored or forgot the fact. I had taught Medical Jurisprudence at Loma Linda University for thirty years, and I assumed that the doctors wanted to hear about the laws governing the practice of medicine. I went to my son's law library and briefed the recent changes in the law, which were very few.

When I found it was a staff meeting of the Catholic hospital I should have refused to speak and suggested a community sing. But I was ready and I was not about to waste a well-prepared lecture.

I had chosen for my subject birth control, abortion, sterilization, monsters, and euthanasia. My granddaughter was a volunteer aide and she was in the dining room. Someone said to her, "Your grandmother is speaking next door."

She replied haughtily, "No, she isn't. People laugh when my grandmother speaks. You don't hear a sound."

The listeners might as well have been painted on the wall. The two nuns who were the hospital administrators sat in the back of the room like two black birds (they have since dropped their habits and issued forth in tweed).

Only one physician laughed and thereby won my undying gratitude.

One of the Catholic doctors present that night was a recent dinner guest. During the evening he remarked, "Mrs. Campbell, do you realize that soon after you made that speech at the hospital, grave doubts were raised in the Catholic Church? We are having our problems."

I thought of the gull who landed on a rock just as there was a great earthquake. The gull looked guilty. He glanced around. "I must be more careful next time I land," he said.

Censorship

JOHN DONNE's last biographer says he wrote "tortuously obscene poems in his youth." I am sorry to hear that. John Donne was a favorite of mine. I prefer to remember him as the fluent dean of St. Paul's.

Pornography vexes me—the very word sounds strangely offensive.

Anthony Comstock was proud to be memorialized by the first law against pornography, and it was a vicious law. He died and left the law to do great harm. I recall a book written by an English doctor, a woman. It was called *Married Love*—a beautiful, sensitive book which might well have been read by every bride. The Comstock law prevented its import into the United States. My own copy came wrapped in the London *Times*.

What a fight was waged for intelligent birth control laws. I knew Margaret Sanger. She was as gentle as a wraith of white smoke and as brave as Daniel. She went to jail eight times, and in her era jails were not the middle-class boardinghouses that they are today. Her only offense was that she gave birth control information to the women in the slums of New York.

So I am wary of censorship. I am wary of any law that attempts to make sin a crime. Freedom is a road, not an inn. The victory is never won. Not all the ills in the world can be corrected by law. Let us revoke the laws against sin so that we can better enforce the laws against crime.

Certainly it was time for a change. Under the aegis of that ill-assorted pair Queen Victoria and Anthony Comstock the facts of life were suppressed and the poor overburdened stork bore his heavy responsibilities for over fifty years.

Thackeray refused to print *Trilby* in the *Cornhill* Magazine. It was thirty years before Gerald du Maurier found a publisher. I read *Trilby* for the first time last winter. Someone must have read it years ago because we had a Jersey cow named Trilby, but the book was never discussed in the family. I found the book quite harmless. Compare it to *Lady Chatterley's Lover*, *Fanny Hill* or the *Decameron*.

The pendulum has swung as far as it will. There is comfort in the hypothetical limit—when things can get no worse they must inexorably get better.

The day will come when a writer no longer finds it necessary to include one vile page to insure publicity. It detracts from a rosy apple to have one rotten spot, no matter how small. A true artist can write the most sordid story without giving offense. Remember *The World of Suzy Wong?*

Readers resent obscenity—"books that shine like dead mackerel in the moonlight and pollute the air around them." The public can be trusted to eventually enforce standards that conform to good breeding and good literature.

I had one unfortunate experience as a censor. My children were allowed to read whatever I read. After I read that mildly objectionable book *Anthony Adverse*, I cut out a few pages before I put it on the library shelf. Kemper Jr. discovered what I had done. "Mother," he asked, "are you compiling a scrapbook?"

My son taught me another lesson. He had a friend whose parents were so strict with him I was afraid they would think Kemper Jr. was a bad influence. One day after visiting his friend for the afternoon he said, "Mother, you have no idea how much worse pictures of naked women are after they have been buried in the back yard."

I hope we will not return to the times of my youth—to ignorance and prudery. Long ago as a young girl at Andrews University I sat on the bank of the St. Joseph River. There were three boys and three girls. It was a Sunday afternoon and one of the boys was reading Elbert Hubbard. He came to the words, "Motherhood and the signs of motherhood should be sacred to every pure-minded young man." The poor boy turned crimson. We were shocked into silence. The conversation stopped on dead center. Finally the oldest girl suggested that we go for a boat ride. No more Elbert Hubbard for us.

Not the Right Solution

A WELL-KNOWN author was being interviewed on television. He was asked for his opinion on the dangers of the population explosion. The man answered that making what Oscar Wilde called "the love that dare not speak its name" both legal and respectable might help. The interviewer quickly changed the subject. No one agrees that this is the answer to the problem.

However, I am glad that England and many of the states have amended their laws, making it a crime only if the young are being corrupted. Laws are passed to protect the innocent from the guilty—it is not their purpose to protect a man from himself. Such laws always fail. No man can be saved against his will, and there should be no laws prohibiting sin, only against crime. There is a valid distinction between them. Leave the battle against sin to the parents, to the schools, to the churches and to a man's own conscience. The government should never be involved.

Laws against sexual perversion only emphasize what they fail to prevent, give publicity to the wrongdoer, arouse curiosity, and make matters worse.

These men live and die under the fixed shadow of censure. 'Tis punishment enough.

I marvel how normal men detect these offenders. My daughter was matron of honor for her closest friend during the war. The bride was one of Lord Balfour's secretaries. In the absence of her father Lord Balfour gave her away. The bride was a well-known tennis player and two tennis players were guests at the wedding. They were the two English civil servants who later defected to Russia.

My son-in-law spotted them immediately. When he came home he said, "Balfour should get rid of those two men. They are not normal and they will do him wrong." Which they did. Their names were McLean and Burgess.

When Kemper came home from Oxford we had a guest who had spent a year in England after graduating from an American college. He retained a touch of soft English accent which I thought was pleasing. I said to my son, "When I visited you in Oxford you spoke so like an English boy I could hardly understand you. This boy was in England only a year. You were there three years and now that you are home you sound just like one of the cowboys."

Kemper gave me a look of utter disgust. "Mama," he said, "if you sent me to England to get an English accent, you wasted ten thousand dollars. There is nothing sillier than an English accent west of the Statue of Liberty. Must I always be telling you the facts of life? Never let that man come to the ranch again."

Six months later I was dining in a restaurant belonging to an English friend. He came to my table and said, "There is someone here I want you to meet." And he took me to where the young man was seated with his mother. He was a lieutenant in the army.

"I know that man. He won't be a lieutenant long," I predicted and walked away. Very shortly thereafter he was out of the army and back in a nearby college.

The rest of the story is well-known for it was a famous murder case.

One evening he picked up a farmhand and gave him a ride into town. The two men went up to his hotel room. Suddenly about nine o'clock the farmhand came rushing down the stairs, half clothed, shouting, "I killed him."

He was arrested and tried for murder. He pled self-defense and the jury acquitted him.

Unknown to Melancholy

I INTRODUCED two new guests this afternoon. Although they had never met before they had one thing in common— the ability to survive every disaster. They should become good friends. One of the few clichés in which I firmly believe is that "misery loves company."

One of them is married to a man with stomach ulcers. Her son has diabetes and her grandson is a spastic and her stepson spends his winters with his mother who has no control over him. He comes west for the summer, bringing all his problems with him.

The other friend married young. Her first husband was a brilliant man but a hopeless alcoholic. One day she packed her three children and drove out of his life. She asked nothing from him. The rest of her story was told to me in confidence, but, without breaking my word, I can truthfully say that she has shown a degree of courage possessed by few women I know. She is about to marry again. She thinks her troubles are over. I fervently hope so. The man she is about to marry is as arbitrary as a stop-and-go signal. Men have invariably complicated her life.

I told these women that I thought Providence was using them for an experiment as he did Job.

The strangest part of this story is that both women are the best of company. We spent a very pleasant afternoon together. I look forward to their visits. They dispel the gloom and leave me determined to stand up to life. I am more than ever persuaded that happiness is not the companion of good fortune but the reward of bedrock courage.

These women were born gay, and gay they will be until death relieves them of the responsibility of being happy.

Joe had a party on his eleventh birthday. I saw a little girl standing in the patio stark and alone. I went to her. "Aren't you having a good time?" I asked. "No," she replied firmly. "Come on, let's find something to do," I suggested. "No," she replied just as stoutly. "I never have a good time at a party."

I met her on the street the other day. She is a grown woman now. I asked her how she was. She told me. She is still grim in her determination to be miserable.

Two Guests

THIS HAS been an eventful day. One guest left and another one came. I had not expected the one to leave nor the other one to return. I was surprised to see her. When she and her husband visited the ranch we did not exchange the usual amenities. He asked what we charged, and when I told him, he said that he had been informed that it was less. I explained that we could no longer take guests for $25 a week. Times had changed. He asked if the pool was heated. I said it was not. Then he wanted to know whether it was warm enough to swim in, and I said, "Not for me." His wife interrupted to say that she did not swim anyway. He asked if we were close enough to town so that his wife could walk that distance since she would not have a car.

"You have just come from town," I replied. "It depends on how far your wife can walk. It is a mile to town but the cemetery is just halfway in case she can't make it."

He left with apparent displeasure. I was reminded of the story of the old New England man who supplemented his income by taking guests for bed and breakfast. One day as he was sitting on his front porch visiting with a neighbor an expensive car drove up. There were two passengers—a chauffeur and a well-dressed woman.

The woman came up the walk and the old man disappeared with her into the house. Suddenly she reappeared and went to the car evidently greatly displeased. The old man came back to his rocking chair.

"What's wrong with her?" the neighbor inquired.

"Nothing," answered the old man.

The neighbor persisted. "She seemed very angry."

"I don't know why," the old man said. "She asked whether we used clean linen and whether we had bugs and I asked her the same question."

So after our interview I did not expect to see either the man or his wife again, but the wife returned. She seems happier alone.

The guest who left this morning left for a strange reason. She said she was lonesome. That is a new complaint. No one has left for that reason before. There are several warm-hearted people with us who are quick to make friends with strangers. I myself sat up with her until eleven o'clock the night she came, listening to her recital of the troubles she had had with doctors, dentists and lawyers. I found it interesting. She is an intelligent, attractive woman. She has spent much time in far places, and she tells her story well.

I was curious. Had she no intimate friends? None in California. We agreed that she needed a few close friends, but she objected to everything I suggested. Unfortunately you cannot go into the marketplace and select a friend exactly to your liking.

I thought about this woman after she left. Perhaps I know the answer to her problem. She showed no interest or curiosity in any of the guests or any member of the family. I do not remember that she asked a single question while she was here.

I compared her to a woman who visits us frequently. She is consumed with curiosity about everyone she meets. I am prepared for a bombardment of questions when she comes. She inquires about every man or woman she has met on the ranch on former visits, which horses are still in the string, are the same girls working for us?

Her questions exhaust me, but she will never be lonely. Put her on a streetcar for Pico, and she will come back with a lifelong friend.

Another answer occurs to me. Did the lonesome guest leave because we have no bar?

One day a respectable-looking woman knocked at the

door. She had two attractive daughters in their early twenties. She inquired about accommodations. Finally she asked if we had a bar. "No, indeed," I answered proudly.

At that she decided not to stay. "Why, with two young daughters, would you want a bar?" I asked in astonishment.

"Where else could they meet men?" she replied.

Remember the Face

I MUST have met close to ten thousand people in Southern California. I try to recall something about those I should remember, but it would be more polite and save any embarrassment if casual acquaintances would introduce themselves first instead of saying, "You don't remember me, do you?" I feel impelled to say, "I'm glad I don't." As Groucho Marx once said, "I never forget a face but I am going to make an exception of yours."

There was a woman who stopped beside my car at a signal. She called to me, "You don't remember me, do you?"

I replied promptly before the signal changed, "I don't remember your name, but I remember that you teach school." Why should she have been displeased?

One day in a crowded elevator in a downtown store a woman made the same remark. "I can't recall your name," I answered, "but I do remember you used to wear De Lisa shoes [a very expensive brand] and you no longer wear them."

It was true. That day she had on a pair of old sandals.

One Last Kindness

THE WOMAN had been coming to the ranch for more than fifteen years. Last summer she phoned to make reservations for a week. She asked for her favorite room—number nine. She had occupied number nine for so many years that she claimed squatters' rights.

We told her another guest was in number nine and we hesitated to ask her to move. We offered her almost any other room in the house.

She was gravely offended. She said it would be "a cold day in Hell" when she came to the ranch again. With this letter, firmly severing our relationship, she enclosed a recipe for a chicken casserole. It is a very good casserole and is popular with both the guests and the family. Perhaps she hoped to be remembered for this last kindness.

Her final injunction was, "Don't give this recipe to any-one east of Chicago." That is why I am prevented from including it in this book.

Wrong Number

SHE HAS a Donald Duck temper. She is conscientious in her search for something to complain about. Pesticides frighten her. She goes shopping around the grocery store with a Geiger counter. The woman's prime target is some public utility. They must have complaint departments for her convenience.

The Western Union especially displeases her because telegrams are not delivered instantaneously. Besides she owns Western Union stock and is entitled to special service.

When she came down to breakfast this morning she looked tired. She had had a bad night. All night long she dreamed that she was trying to call her daughter on the telephone. She was never successful. The lines were either busy or central gave her the wrong number. It was very annoying.

"I must report it to the telephone company," she said.

It wouldn't surprise me if she kept her word.

I Know a Secret

FEW SECRETS can be kept forever. Once told they are easier to forget.

I have wanted to tell this story for years. I hope Ray Milland will not mind.

When Joe was about ten years old he asked me if he could have a clip haircut. It was a hot summer so I gave my permission. Whatever it was Joe wanted it was not what he got. The barber called me and said that Joe was so embarrassed he did not want to come home. When I found him he looked like Yul Brynner although it was long before Mr. Brynner made the style popular.

The next morning at the breakfast table I said to Joe, "I never worry about a haircut. Your hair will grow out quickly. But never come home with a tattoo. A tattoo lasts a lifetime."

Ray Milland was sitting beside Joe. "That's right," he said. He pulled up his sleeve and displayed a skull with a serpent's head emerging from an eye socket.

"Who would ever select that design!" I exclaimed in horror.

"No one," Ray answered. "I thought it was a rose until I woke up the next morning."

The Blue Carpet

ONE OF my best friends has done very well selling carpet in San Francisco. It was he who carpeted Gold Street in Chinatown from sidewalk to sidewalk.

More than once he had carpeted the entire Palace Hotel. Six years ago he was given the order to do it again, and the contract specified that the carpet was to be blue. After the carpet was ordered—six thousand dollars' worth—the hotel changed hands, and the new owner could not abide the color blue.

My friend told me about it, and I asked him whether he would sue for the amount due him. His reply was exactly what I expected, "Under no circumstances." The man who originally ordered the carpet had been a good friend for many years. There are some lawsuits you cannot afford to win. What you make on the swings you lose on the roundabouts.

So for six years I have been inquiring about that blue carpet. The loss of the contract did not affect my friend's disposition nor his golf game. I have seen him far more disturbed when he missed a putt.

It became well known on the ranch that he had blue carpet for sale. Little by little he disposed of it in small allotments. The roll diminished slowly.

Yesterday my friend came for his summer visit. I asked the same question. "How about the blue carpet?"

His face lighted up. "I sold the last of it yesterday, and let me tell you a funny thing. The man who ordered it in the first place bought it. The city was demolishing the building where he had his office and he bought it for his new office. That blue carpet was worth ten thousand dollars in good public relations."

These are not for sale in supermarkets—good friends, good reputations and integrity. Be wary of the ultimate dollar.

In Her Garden

A GARDEN has a long memory. A garden remembers when friends forget. In the spring, they say, flowers still bloom in the garden of Gethsemane.

This morning I walked down the hill to her cottage below the main house. Her garden has not yet heard the sad news that she is gone. The chrysanthemums, the gaillardias, the clematis and the tuberoses are all in bloom as though nothing had happened.

She was the youngest of the three. I was the oldest. Now there are only two. There never were any more. How can Easter come again? It was at Easter that we were always together.

The three weeks of her illness cast a long, long shadow. She could not speak, she could not move, she could not eat.

She could only communicate with her wide brown eyes and the help of the alphabet.

She did not want to live. Twice she told this to the doctor. There was no doubt about what she meant. He said he could keep her alive for a long time. She would have none of it. Without tears she chose to die.

I shall always remember her few messages. She said she did not want a special nurse nor a private room. Would someone brush her hair? Please bring a light bulb so that the night nurse could read while she slept. Open the window so that she could see the garden outside. Take away the wilted flowers and bring water for the fresh ones. No farewells— no dramatics. Twice I saw tears in her eyes. Once when Joe spoke of O.J. She was so proud of him. I cannot remember that since 1934 she ever missed a football game when her college was playing at home. Someone must wonder where the little old woman who knew all the players and all the plays has gone.

And she wept when a cousin came to see her. They were both widowed and had shared their joys and sorrows. She had helped this cousin raise two fine sons. When she saw her she spelled out the words, "I am crying because I am happy." God gave her the will to die with dignity.

She was a well-known orthodontist. She had lived long enough to have her patients send her their own children. Daniel Pollock, the famous pianist, was her devoted friend and patient. He came from New York to play "Jesu Joy of Man's Desiring" and Liszt's "Consolation" at her funeral.

When she retired she could say that she never turned a

child away because he was too poor to pay for her services.

I love the story of the little newsboy who sold her the evening papers. One day she said to him, "You need to have your teeth straightened. If you will come to my office and keep your appointments faithfully I will straighten your teeth for five dollars a month." The boy was prompt and honest.

When he came with the last five dollars she said, "I always make a reduction for cash. You don't owe me any more money." And she gave him back the five dollars.

Outside Budapest there is a cemetery and over the gate are the words (interpreted), "In God's knowing there are no whys."

The Wonder of Words

MY MOTHER never corrected us when we mispronounced a word. She waited for an occasion to pronounce the word properly. She was afraid to discourage us in the use of unfamiliar words.

I once had a friend who went through life on words of one syllable. She made out very well since many of these words have an exact meaning, but she had one unpleasant habit. If anyone in her presence used a word in a higher bracket, she would ask, "Is that the way you pronounce it?" There is no surer way to reduce conversation to its bare essentials.

When my older son was twenty-two months old I recorded his vocabulary. He used one thousand different words in the space of two weeks. So far as I know this is still a record. I counted my daughter's vocabulary at two years—she used over seven hundred words which is exceptionally good.

Alas, at two years the younger son made do with twenty words. I was frightened. I told his father it was wise to have no more children. The next child might well be speechless.

Now I know the answer. We had a maid with a son exactly Joe's age. They were constant companions from the time they were a year old until they were ten. One was black and one was white. They had a perfect understanding, a language of their own. They had no need to communicate with the rest of us. It turned out that Joe became the master of the adequate word. This should prove something.

When my two older children were planning to go to school in Europe, one to Paris and one to Oxford, I spent one winter improving their use of words. I said, "I have bought your luggage. You are planning your wardrobe. Your father will buy the tickets, but you need a better vocabulary."

Every weekend during the winter they each brought me a list of ten words—not long or unusual but words to be used in daily intelligent conversation. Their father gave a prize for the best list. And on Saturday morning I reread the accumulated list of words to them.

My reward is that my family enjoy words as they enjoy good food and becoming clothes. It is a pleasure to listen to my grandchildren. They are never frustrated or misunderstood for lack of the right word.

I take delight in words, but alas, there are some words which do not become me. I have to be careful, just as there are colors I cannot wear—yellow for instance, and I like yellow. I cannot use the word "empathy"—I have to be satisfied with sympathy. And there is that lovely word "serendipity." It does not belong to me. And so with "chauvinistic" and "horrendous," and many other words. They are not for me. When I use them they lose their meaning and are stumbling blocks in the path of the reader.

I should be very proud to have invented a useful word, but this is seldom possible. One of my friends invented a word which fills a widespread need. What does one say when he steps out of the shower to find that the towel he had carefully hung in its place has vanished leaving no trace? There is no single word to cover the situation. But now through the courtesy of this friend we have the word "exeem" which is the opposite of the word "exist." It is a very useful word and there are far too many times when it is needed. It is less exasperating if there is a word to cover one's annoyance.

I hope the word will be accepted in everyday conversation and achieve a place in the dictionary if not in Fowler's *Modern English Usage*.

A Word of Farewell: A Flawless Friendship

THEY BURIED him today on the north side of the hill next to his cousin who was lost in the Second World War. It was where he wanted to be. The ranch was always home to him.

I met him first on my wedding trip. I had married his uncle and stopped overnight in Fresno to visit his family. Dick was three years old. He sat in a big chair across the room and studied me with his clear blue eyes. Then he came over and stood beside me. It was the beginning of a flawless friendship.

When he graduated from college I offered to send him to law school, but he chose the open skies instead of the eleventh floor of an office building. I have his answer to my offer. It is one of the letters that have made my life plausible. "Thank you," he wrote. "You are the only relative I have who has given me anything but love."

Somewhere among his papers he has preserved my answer. "I am disappointed. There will come a day when it will be a grey plane under a grey sky over a grey ocean, and I will never know what happened to you." I was wrong: he died in a hotel in Madrid at fifty-six.

He was a commercial pilot for thirty-four years with a perfect record.

How much I received in return for the little I gave him!

When Kemper Jr. died he took a month's leave of absence and came to occupy Kemper's room next to mine.

Once when life became too complicated I called him long distance. "Be at the airport at five o'clock," he said. "I am checking out a pilot on a Constellation and I will meet you there." It was so long ago that there was only a fence between the planes and waiting relatives.

I was standing by the barrier when the Tower announced that the Hawaiian Clipper was arriving early. I was always inclined to be an exhibitionist. I turned to the waiting crowd and said, "It is not the Hawaiian Clipper. It is just my nephew coming in from San Francisco to visit me."

The great white bird circled the field and landed directly in front of us. Dick, dispatch case in hand, came down the steps alone and we walked away arm in arm. It was one of my proudest moments.

Just before he left on his last trip he wrote to his close friend John Wayne. He was referring to an incident that happened when John Wayne was a guest at the ranch. His letter ended with his final tribute, "My Aunt Litta Belle is still my very favorite person in the world."

There is no one left now who thinks I can do no wrong. Dick and my grandmother are both gone. It makes for a lonesome world.